Armies of Dark Ages Europe, 613–987

Gabriele Esposito is a military historian who works as a freelance author and researcher for some of the most important publishing houses in the military history sector. In particular, he is an expert specializing in uniformology: his interests and expertise range from the ancient civilizations to modern post-colonial conflicts. During recent years, he has conducted and published several researches on the military history of the Latin American countries, with special attention on the War of the Triple Alliance and the War of the Pacific. He is among the leading experts on the military history of the Italian Wars of Unification and the Spanish Carlist Wars. His books and essays are published on a regular basis by Osprey Publishing, Winged Hussar Publishing and Libreria Editrice Goriziana. He is also the author of numerous military history articles appearing in specialized magazines such as *Ancient Warfare Magazine*, *Medieval Warfare Magazine*, *The Armourer*, *History of War*, *Guerres et Histoire*, *Focus Storia* and *Focus Storia Wars*.

Armies of Dark Ages Europe, 613–987

Charlemagne, the Carolingians and their Enemies

Gabriele Esposito

Pen & Sword
MILITARY

First published in Great Britain in 2024 by
Pen & Sword Military
An imprint of
Pen & Sword Books Limited
Yorkshire – Philadelphia

ISBN 978 1 39903 191 2

A CIP catalogue record for this book is available from the British Library

Typeset by Mac Style
Printed and bound in India by Replika Press Pvt Ltd.

Pen & Sword Books Limited incorporates the imprints of After the Battle, Atlas, Archaeology, Aviation, Discovery, Family History, Fiction, History, Maritime, Military, Military Classics, Politics, Select, Transport, True Crime, Air World, Frontline Publishing, Leo Cooper, Remember When, Seaforth Publishing, The Praetorian Press, Wharncliffe Local History, Wharncliffe Transport, Wharncliffe True Crime and White Owl.

For a complete list of Pen & Sword titles please contact:

PEN & SWORD BOOKS LIMITED
47 Church Street, Barnsley, South Yorkshire, S70 2AS, England
E-mail: enquiries@pen-and-sword.co.uk
Website: www.pen-and-sword.co.uk
or
PEN AND SWORD BOOKS
1950 Lawrence Rd, Havertown, PA 19083, USA
E-mail: uspen-and-sword@casematepublishers.com
Website: www.penandswordbooks.com

Contents

Acknowledgements vi
Introduction vii

Chapter 1 The Birth of Germanic Europe, AD 200–476 1

Chapter 2 The Romano-Germanic Kingdoms, 476–613 27

Chapter 3 The Ascendancy of the Carolingians, 613–768 86

Chapter 4 The Wars of Charlemagne, 768–814 96

Chapter 5 The Carolingian Army 112

Chapter 6 The Decline of the Carolingians, 814–987 131

Chapter 7 The Viking Menace, 799–987 151

Chapter 8 Weapons and Tactics 167

Bibliography 189
The Re-enactors who Contributed to this Book 190
Index 195

Acknowledgements

This book is dedicated to my magnificent parents, Maria Rosaria and Benedetto, for the immense love and fundamental support that they always give me. Thanks to their precious advice deriving from long experience, the present book has turned out even better than I had envisaged. A very special thanks goes to Philip Sidnell, the commissioning editor of my books for Pen & Sword: his love for history and his passion for publishing are the key factors behind the success of our publications. Many thanks also to the production manager of this title, Matt Jones, for his excellent work and great enthusiasm. Special thanks are due to Tony Walton for editing my original manuscript in his usual considered and informed manner. A very special mention goes to the brilliant re-enactment groups that collaborated with their photographs to the creation of this book: without the incredible work of research of their members, the final result of this publication would not have been the same. As a result, I want to express my deep gratitude to the following living history associations/single re-enactors: De vita aetate carolingorum from Germany, Harjaz Toringem – IG frühgeschichtliche Kulturen from Germany, Hiwisca – Eine Familia in der Karolingerzeit from Germany, Projekt Deutschritter from Germany, Gisna Missi Dominici from France, Lupi Austrasiae from France, Viatores from France, Bert Tessens from Belgium and Novum Milites Francorum from the Netherlands.

Introduction

The decades that followed the fall of the Western Roman Empire in AD 476 saw the formation of Germanic Europe, a new Europe comprising the Romano-Germanic kingdoms that emerged from the fusion between different Germanic communities and the Roman population. Over time, one such Romano-Germanic realm, the Frankish Kingdom, came to dominate over all the others and conquered most of continental Europe under the guidance of the Carolingian royal family. In this book, we will follow the military ascendancy of the warlike Franks from 613 – the year during which the future Carolingian dynasty rose to prominence in the Frankish Kingdom – to the disappearance of the last Carolingians in 987. The great protagonist of this bloody historical period was undoubtedly Charlemagne, probably the greatest military commander of the Early Middle Ages. He transformed the Frankish Kingdom into a massive state – the Holy Roman Empire – that dominated most of continental Western Europe for almost a century. Charlemagne spent his long reign (768–814) fighting against a multitude of warlike enemies who lived on the frontiers of his dominions: Arabs, Basques, Bretons, Frisians, Vikings, Saxons, Thuringians, Slavs, Avars, Bavarians and Lombards. He obtained many spectacular victories over these peoples, but also suffered some humiliating defeats, such as that at Roncevaux Pass. We will follow the evolution of the Frankish army from the rise of the Franks under the Merovingian monarchs to the dissolution of the Carolingian Empire, reconstructing the most important military campaigns in detail. All the major troop types will be covered, providing information on the organization and equipment of the various contingents. The enemies of the Franks will also be examined, thereby providing a much fuller and more rounded picture of the era. As the following pages will reveal, the years 613–987 were fundamental in determining the identity of Europe in the Middle Ages and witnessed the emergence of various long-lasting institutions that were forged by war. It is believed by many modern historians that the era examined by this book is known as the Dark Ages because there is not a great amount of recorded information about the time, with little detailed light thus shone on this period of European history. The more traditional view was that Dark Ages referred to the 'darkness' of the early medieval period compared to the 'lightness' of the previous age of classical antiquity.

Chapter 1

The Birth of Germanic Europe, AD 200–476

Around AD 200, several new Germanic tribes appeared on the north-eastern borders of the Roman Empire. These were all migrating from Eastern Europe and, after having settled in eastern Germany, were starting to exert an increasing pressure over the Germanic communities that had long inhabited western Germany. Several of the new Germanic groups coming into contact with the Romans were not 'tribes' in the classical sense of the term, but conglomerations of tribes that comprised many smaller communities. The most important of these was the Alamanni, whose name meant 'all men' and who fought for the first time against the Romans during the reign of Emperor Caracalla (AD 213). The Alamanni attacked the Roman frontier in its most exposed area: the *Agri Decumates* (Decumatian Fields). This region was located in present-day south-western Germany and linked up the *limes* (or frontier) of the Rhine with that of the Danube. The Decumatian Fields were the only place in continental Europe where the border of the Roman Empire was not marked by the mighty barriers of the Rhine or the Danube, so they were particularly exposed to foreign invasions and had thus been heavily fortified by the Romans. By conquering the Decumatian Fields, an enemy of Rome could easily outflank the defences of the Rhine in the north west or those of the Danube in the south-east. The Alamanni settled just outside the Roman fortifications of the Decumatian Fields and started to attack them during the early decades of the third century. In AD 235, Emperor Severus Alexander was assassinated by his own soldiers while campaigning against the Alamanni, leading to the beginning of the 'Crisis of the Third Century', which came very near to causing the fall of the Roman Empire. Since its creation, the Roman state had never experienced such a complex and multi-factorial crisis. All aspects of life in the Roman Empire were affected by it: political, economic and social. Foreign invasions and internal secessions were key elements of the crisis, which saw the Alamanni conquering the Decumatian Fields in AD 260 and the secession of all the western provinces of the Empire. These provinces, comprising Iberia and Gaul, in addition to Britain, proclaimed their independence from Rome as the Gallic Empire and started to fight in an autonomous way against the Germani.

In such a situation, characterized by enormous political chaos, other Germanic conglomerations appeared on the borders of the Roman state. These included the

Ostrogoth heavy infantryman equipped with helmet and chainmail. (*Photo by Sebastian Wesche-Bachmann, copyright by Franz Kanschberger*)

Visigoth warrior wearing short-sleeved chainmail. (*Photo and copyright by Viatores*)

Gepid warrior armed with *angon* heavy javelin and sword.
(*Photo by Sebastian Wesche-Bachmann, copyright by Cristoph Todte*)

Franks, who settled on the eastern bank of the Rhine and had as their main objective the invasion of Gaul. The Roman military situation in the West remained extremely difficult when the secession of the Gallic Empire was crushed, due to the presence of the Alamanni and the Franks. Meanwhile, in the eastern provinces, the relative stability of the early third century was soon menaced by the arrival of the most important of all the Germanic conglomerations, the Goths. The latter, the most numerous of the eastern Germani, had lived for many decades in the plains of modern Poland and Ukraine (not far from the Volga River). Now, coming under strong pressure from the warlike peoples of Central Asia, they wanted to cross the Danube and establish their new homeland south of the great river. Initially, the Roman authorities tried to find a compromise with the Goths, paying them in exchange for providing military contingents that would serve in the Roman army. This was the beginning of a new process that would see the progressive 'barbarization' of the Roman army, which started to comprise an increasing number of Germanic soldiers whose loyalty towards Rome was far from stable and who were commanded by their own officers. For a variety of reasons, including the diffusion of the new Christian religion, the Roman manpower available for the military forces of the Empire was rapidly decreasing, so the Imperial authorities had no choice but to employ an increasing number of barbarians to fill the gaps in their armies. These Germanic soldiers could be recruited as single mercenaries (*bucellarii*) or as warriors who were part of an allied community (*foederati*). Sometimes, in exchange for their military services, the *foederati* were permitted to settle inside the borders of the Empire in order to act as farmers and soldiers. This new system, however, soon showed its limitations, producing an increasing fragmentation of Roman territory.

In AD 250, the Goths, together with the Carpi and other Germanic groups, broke the Roman defences on the Danube and invaded the Balkan provinces of the Empire. The Germani successfully besieged Philippopolis and then defeated a large Roman force at the Battle of Abritus. This clash took place south of the Danube and ended in disaster for the Romans: Emperor Decius, who was in command of the three legions that tried to stop the Goths, was killed and his army was routed. After this great victory, the Goths returned north of the Danube after signing a peace treaty which humiliated the Romans: the Germani were permitted to take with them all the goods that they had plundered in the Balkans, while Rome was to pay a yearly tribute to them in order to preserve its territorial integrity. The bloody campaigns fought between the Romans and the Germani during the third century were completely different from those of earlier times, as the Germani were now migrating towards the Empire and thus did not limit themselves to conducting rapid incursions. They had no fear of the Romans and did not refrain from confronting them on the open field. It

Thuringian warrior equipped with spangenhelm and *angon*.
(*Photo by Sebastian Wesche-Bachmann, copyright by Sebastian Wesche-Bachmann*)

Herulian warlord. Note the magnificent manufacture of his helmet and sword. (*Photo by Sebastian Wesche-Bachmann, copyright by Rene Wissendorf Christoffersen*)

Ostrogoth warrior wearing a superb example of a spangenhelm. (*Photo by Sebastian Wesche-Bachmann, copyright by Maximilian Streibl*)

should be noted that the eastern Germani had some military peculiarities compared with their western compatriots: having been in close contact with the steppe peoples, they had introduced heavy cavalry and archers into their military forces. These two elements had never been a major part of the Germanic armies that had fought against the Romans during the previous centuries. With the fall of the Decumatian Fields, the Alamanni and the Franks started to launch frequent raids along the western bank of the Rhine. Meanwhile, new groups such as the Vandals and the Burgundians also appeared along the *limes* in search of new lands. After Diocletian's ascendancy in AD 284, the Roman Empire was completely reorganized from an administrative point of view and a degree of stability was restored. Under Constantine the Great, the Roman army was reformed, leading to a general improvement in the situation along the borders of the Empire. Germanic attacks were repulsed for several decades, but these Roman successes were only postponing the inevitable. After Constantine's death (AD 337), the Empire became involved in a series of violent civil wars between the heirs of the emperor. These conflicts featured the participation of an increasing number of Germanic warriors, both mercenary and allied.

During the 350s, Emperor Julian campaigned against the Alamanni and the Franks on the Rhine. Despite crushing them in a decisive battle at Strasbourg (AD 357), he had to accept the presence of some Frankish communities on the territory of the Empire. After the Battle of Strasbourg, Julian was able to restore the Roman defences of the Rhine frontier, even launching several punitive raids against the Germanic tribes. Some of these tribes were forced to become *tributarii* (vassals) of Rome and started to pay an annual tribute to the Empire. A few years after his success against the Alamanni, Julian launched a massive campaign against the Sassanid Persians in the Middle East. This ended in complete failure, with the death of Julian and the loss of many troops who would have been fundamental for the defence of the Empire. A few years after Julian's death, all the improvements obtained thanks to the victory at Strasbourg had been lost and Gaul was again plundered by the Germani. In AD 369, the Romans abandoned their province of Dacia, which was extremely difficult to defend since it was located north of the Danube. By AD 376, the Goths had entered Roman territory in great numbers. By that time, the Roman state was already divided into two parts, each of which was ruled by an autonomous emperor: the Western Empire and the Eastern Empire. Being pressed by the Huns, who were moving from the steppes of Central Asia, many thousands of Goths camped north of the Danube and asked the local Roman authorities (of the Eastern Empire) permission to cross the river in order to settle in the Balkans. Valens, at that time the emperor of the Eastern Empire, welcomed the Goths as *foederati* and permitted them to cross the Danube. Valens intended them to act as military colonists and defend the eastern portion of the Danubian *limes* on behalf of Rome. The Goths, however, were treated very badly by the Roman officials who supervised their settlement, with the Germani not receiving the promised food and being forced to live in a state of misery.

In consequence of these events, the Goths rebelled against the Romans and started to plunder the provinces located south of the Danube in search of new lands where they could settle. In AD 378, after some minor and indecisive clashes, Valens marched at the head of his army against the Goths. The Romans built a strong fortified camp near the city of Adrianople before moving against the Goths, who were encamped not far from the Roman positions. The Germani, led by Fritigern, had their families and their wagons with them as they were migrating across the Balkans. After a difficult march under the sun, the Roman soldiers were tired and dehydrated when they reached the enemy camp. The Goths responded by forming a defensive circle with their wagons and placing their infantry inside it, while the cavalry operated independently. The Germanic camp was built on top of a hill and was thus a good defensive position. In order to harass the Romans and delay their advance, the Goths set fire to the fields surrounding the hill. The Gothic cavalry was away from the battlefield, conducting a foraging expedition, so Fritigern needed to gain time before the Romans attacked his positions. Eventually, without receiving any precise orders from their commander, the Roman soldiers attacked the Goths without coordination and were easily repulsed. When it seemed that they might nevertheless break through the Gothic defences, Fritigern's cavalry appeared on the battlefield and charged into the rear of the attackers. Surrounded, the Romans were completely routed, Valens being killed together with many of his soldiers. After the Battle of Adrianople, the Goths established a stable presence inside the borders of the Roman Empire, by now being too strong to be defeated. The following decades saw the outbreak of fresh civil wars within the Roman Empire, culminating in the Battle of the Frigidus River (AD 394). This clash was fought between the Western Empire of the usurper Eugenius (who supported pagan polytheism) and the Eastern Empire of Emperor Theodosius I (who supported Christian monotheism). The battle, probably the bloodiest in the history of the Late Empire, saw the participation of thousands of Germanic warriors who fought with both armies. The Eastern Empire, for example, deployed a powerful contingent of 20,000 Goths, while the Western Empire had a significant number of Frankish warriors. The clash took place in modern Slovenia, not far from the border that separated the Western and Eastern Empires. It resulted in a decisive victory for Theodosius I and his Christian faith, Eugenius being killed and his army completely destroyed. After the Battle of the Frigidus River, the military forces of the Western Empire practically ceased to exist, opening the way for the subsequent invasions that caused its fall.

Thuringian warrior armed with spear, sword, knife and *francisca* throwing axe. (*Photo by Sebastian Wesche-Bachmann, copyright by Sebastian Wesche-Bachmann*)

Bavarian warrior equipped with spear and round shield. (*Photo by Sebastian Wesche-Bachmann, copyright by Tobias Eisenkolb*)

Saxon warrior armed with *seax* short sword.
(*Photo by Sebastian Wesche-Bachmann, copyright by Stephan Becker*)

Theodosius I died in AD 395, after which the Roman Empire was definitively divided between his two young sons: the eastern portion was given to the older son, Arcadius, with the western half going to his younger brother, Honorius. Following these events, two Germanic warlords assumed indirect control over the Roman state as both Arcadius and Honorius were too young to rule without a regent: Stilicho ruled in the Western Empire and Alaric in the Eastern Empire. Stilicho, a half Vandal who had married the niece of Theodosius I, became the regent of Honorius, while Alaric, a Goth, was appointed *magister militum* (supreme military commander) by Arcadius. After the Battle of the Frigidus River and the subsequent ascendancy of Alaric, the Gothic communities divided themselves into two main groups: the Visigoths, or Western Goths, and Ostrogoths, or Eastern Goths. The Visigoths, whose first monarch was Alaric, consisted of those Goths who already lived inside the borders of the Roman Empire and had culturally already been partly 'romanized'. The Ostrogoths, meanwhile, were those Goths who were starting to migrate south of the Danube and were still strongly influenced by the culture of the steppe peoples. Around AD 400, the Ostrogoths came under increasing pressure from the Huns and started to move in great numbers towards Roman lands, together with several other groups of eastern Germani who were allies or subjects of the Huns. This huge migratory movement caused the final collapse of the Western Empire, which was already crumbling under the attacks of other Germanic tribes such as the Alamanni and the Franks.

During his early career, Stilicho served with distinction under Theodosius I and rapidly became one of the most important generals of the Roman army. After participating in the Battle of the Frigidus River, he was appointed by the emperor as guardian of the young Honorius. Alaric, as overlord of the Goths, also fought at the Frigidus River, where he met Stilicho for the first time. During the following years, the two 'barbarian' generals fought each other in a series of violent wars. After the death of Theodosius, Alaric hoped to become the guardian of Arcadius and obtain a leading political role in the administration of the Eastern Empire, but he was prevented from doing so by the ascendancy of Stilicho and reacted by invading the Balkans with his warriors. Alaric rapidly advanced south and was able to raid through most of Greece without encountering any serious opposition. The Eastern Empire was in a state of complete chaos at this time, with opposing political factions trying to influence the young Arcadius. In AD 397, seeing that the situation in the east was becoming desperate, Stilicho landed in Greece and defeated the Visigoths in Arcadia. Alaric, however, escaped capture and continued to ravage the Balkans until he was finally appointed *magister militum* by Arcadius. From AD 398–400, Stilicho had to fight against the Picts in northern Britain and crush an internal rebellion in northern Africa. Alaric, meanwhile, started planning an invasion of Italy. In AD 402, Alaric's Visigoths launched their attack, but they were defeated by Stilicho at the Battle of Pollentia in northern Italy. This was a severe blow for Alaric, whose wife was captured by Stilicho and who lost most of his best warriors. The Battle of Pollentia was the last military victory for which a triumph was celebrated in Rome. In AD 405, a major invasion of Italy was launched by a coalition of Germanic tribes, including the Vandals. Against the odds, Stilicho was able to repulse the invasion, despite his forces being outnumbered. Within months of his victory, however, the great Germanic general received worrying news from the frontier of Gaul, where a large number of Germani had crossed the Rhine and were devastating Roman territories located north of the Alps.

While these events took place on the *limes*, the usurper Constantine III revolted in Britain and seceded from the Western Empire. Being unable to deal with the worsening military situation, Stilicho lost the support of both the Roman Senate and his troops. His forces mutinied in AD 408 and organized a coup, which was instigated by Stilicho's political rivals and ended with his execution. Following Stilicho's death, Italy spiralled into chaos, the local population massacring thousands of Germanic women and children from the families of the *foederati* soldiers who operated in Italy. Presenting himself as the defender of the Germani, Alaric invaded Italy for a second time and besieged the city of Rome. After a siege lasting two years, during which he tried to obtain significant territorial concessions for his Visigoths from the Senate, Alaric occupied Rome. Hunger was the most powerful weapon of the Germanic warriors besieging the city, whose inhabitants lacked sufficient food reserves and had to resort to cannibalism in order to survive. Alaric's siege of Rome was not a continuous one, consisting of three separate shorter sieges that took place over a period of two years. The Western Empire no longer had an effective military force that could expel the Visigoths from Italy, meaning the Germanic warriors were free to move around the peninsula. In AD 410, Alaric's men finally entered Rome and sacked the city. However, despite the fears of the Romans, they did not commit any atrocities and did not kill any civilians. Just a few buildings were burned and all the properties of the Christian Church were spared. Alaric still wanted to present himself as a Roman official rather than a cruel barbarian invader. Shortly after seizing Rome, he moved south towards Sicily with the intention of invading northern Africa, where the grain needed by Italy was produced. During the crossing of the strait that connects mainland Italy with Sicily, however, the fleet of the Visigoths was battered by a storm. Alaric died a few days after this unfortunate event, probably of a fever.

In AD 423, Emperor Honorius died, having been unable to defend Rome from the invasion of the Visigoths and to preserve the territorial integrity of the Western

Ostrogoth warrior wearing soft Phrygian cap. (*Photo by Sebastian Wesche-Bachmann, copyright by Maximilian Streibl*)

Frankish warrior equipped with spear and round shield. (*Photo and copyright by Bert Tessens*)

Empire. His death caused the outbreak of a new civil war, with a usurper known as Joannes proclaimed emperor in the west while the eastern monarch, Theodosius II (son of Arcadius, who had died), appointed his cousin, Valentinian, as western emperor. This civil war ended when an expeditionary corps from the east invaded Italy and deposed Joannes, who died in AD 425. As a result, Valentinian became supreme ruler of the west and started to exert his power from Ravenna (the new capital of the Western Empire), together with his ambitious and intelligent mother, Galla Placidia. During the civil war that ended with the ascendancy of Valentinian, Joannes sent one of his best military officers to the lands of the Huns with orders to raise a large force of Hunnic warriors and to return to Italy as soon as possible in order to fight against the soldiers of the Eastern Empire. This officer was Flavius Aetius, an intelligent and capable commander who had spent most of his early life as a hostage at the court of the Hunnic kings. When Aetius returned to Italy with the force of Hunnic warriors, he learned that the civil war was over and that his overlord, Joannes, had been defeated. Consequently, he had no choice but to find a compromise with

Thuringian warrior armed with spear, sword and *seax*. (*Photo and copyright Martin Just*)

Valentinian. He was appointed *magister militum per Gallias*, assuming control over an important portion of the Western Empire. Aetius ruled Gaul as an independent monarch, as Valentinian and Galla Placidia did not have the military resources to protect the frontier of the Rhine. By that time, several Germanic tribes had settled permanently in Gaul and the whole region was in a state of chaos: the Rhine was no longer a military barrier and the emperors of the west exerted their authority only over the city of Ravenna. Despite all these difficulties, Aetius did his best to assume effective control over Gaul by using military power as well as diplomacy. Soon after taking overall command of the Roman troops in Gaul, Aetius obtained a series of victories over the Visigoths and the Franks. The Visigoths had settled in southern France, while the Franks had occupied large portions of territory on the western bank of the Rhine. The Roman general was not able to expel the Germani from Gaul, but confined them in small areas of territory where their movements could be controlled. Between AD 433 and 450, thanks to his victories, Flavius Aetius became the dominant military and political personality of the Western Empire: he was formally appointed as the 'protector' of Valentinian and continued to fight successfully against the Germani in Gaul. Aetius defeated the Visigoths again and forced them to form a military alliance with him in exchange for receiving permission to remain in Gaul. In addition, he crushed the Germanic tribe of the Burgundians who had crossed the Rhine some years before and were now forced to settle on a limited portion of territory. By the time of Aetius' victories in Gaul, the Romans had already evacuated Britain (AD 410) and had lost any form of control over the Iberian Peninsula (where the Vandals had settled).

Due to his personal relations with important members of the Hunnic court, Aetius was always able to deploy significant numbers of Hunnic warriors. By AD 450, the Huns had created an immense multinational empire that comprised a large portion of Central Asia as well as most of Eastern Europe. They had already attacked and defeated the forces of the Eastern Empire and were now ready to invade the rich territories of Gaul. Although Aetius, thanks to his diplomatic skills, had formed a strong alliance with the Huns, this vanished when a new leader emerged among the nomads of the steppes: Attila. Extremely ambitious, Attila wanted to become the supreme ruler of the Western Empire, as a result of which he soon started planning an attack against Gaul. The invasion materialized in AD 451, when Attila crossed the Rhine with a large multinational army. The Huns were completely different from both the Romans and the Germani; they were incredibly ferocious and had the best cavalry of the known world. Armed with composite bows and mounted on small ponies, they seemed to be invincible. The Germani were literally terrorized by the Huns, probably more so than the Romans. The eastern Germani tribes had

Frankish swordsman. (*Photo and copyright by Bert Tessens*)

already fought against Attila's warriors during the previous decades and had been soundly defeated. As a result, when the Huns began to threaten Gaul, Aetius did not have great difficulties in forming a Romano-Germanic military coalition to face Attila. By that time, the Romans and the Germani had found some form of mutual equilibrium in Gaul, which risked being destroyed by the Huns. If the Huns occupied the Western Empire, the Germanic peoples living in Gaul would have been obliged to abandon the new homelands for which they had fought for years. Aetius thus established a large military alliance that comprised Romans, Visigoths, Salian Franks, Burgundians, Saxons and Alans. The Alans were not a Germanic group, but a steppe people who had migrated towards Gaul with the Germani before being

Thuringian warrior armed with thrusting axe. Note the soft cap resembling the Late Roman *pileus pannonicus*. (*Photo by Sebastian Wesche-Bachmann, copyright by Cristoph Todte*)

Frankish warrior equipped with massive sword and top-quality *seax*. (*Photo and copyright by Bert Tessens*)

submitted by Aetius. The Hunnic army of Attila was made up of contingents from a large portion of Eastern Europe: Ostrogoths, Rugians, Scirii, Thuringians, Ripuarian Franks, Gepids and Heruli.

The decisive clash between these two coalitions took place in AD 451 and is commonly known as the Battle of the Catalaunian Plains. After entering Gaul, the Hunnic army besieged the city of Aurelianum (modern Orléans). Aetius moved towards the city before the invaders could occupy it, and the decisive battle was fought not far from Orléans. From an ethnic point of view, the Battle of the Catalaunian Plains could be defined as a clash between the western Germani and the eastern Germani. After several hours of fierce fighting, the western Germani prevailed and Flavius Aetius secured victory over Attila. During the clash, the Visigoths and the Ostrogoths fought against each other with incredible violence, revealing that inter-tribal hate was still a fundamental component of the Germanic civilization. The king of the Visigoths, the great warlord Theodoric, was killed by the Ostrogoths during the battle. The direct consequences of the clash on the Catalaunian Plains were extremely important for the history of Western Europe: we could only imagine what could have happened if the Huns had prevailed and occupied all of Gaul. In AD 452, having reorganized his forces, Attila attacked the Western Empire again and ravaged most of northern Italy before going back to his main base in Europe, which was located in Pannonia (modern Hungary). The Hunnic warlord was assassinated during the following year, his immense empire soon crumbling after the outbreak of a civil war which was fought to determine the identity of his successor. With the death of Attila, Emperor Valentinian, becoming increasingly worried about the power of Aetius, organized a plot against him. In AD 453, the great Roman general was assassinated, the Western Empire thereby losing its last capable military commander. With Aetius' death, it was just a question of time before Rome would be sacked again. Valentinian was killed by one of Aetius' Hunnic bodyguards and the Empire soon entered a new and chaotic political phase. In AD 455, the Vandals, under their king Genseric, landed near Rome and sacked the city. Once again, the sack was not particularly violent, but the Vandals looted as much as possible, meaning the old capital of the Empire was reduced to an impoverished city. In AD 476, the military leader of the Germanic *foederati* stationed in Italy, Odoacer of the Scirii, deposed the last monarch of the Western Empire (the young Romolus Augustulus). The glory of the Roman Empire was over and a new historical phase – dominated by the Germanic peoples – had begun for Western Europe.

Frankish light infantryman armed with *angon* javelin. (*Photo and copyright by Bert Tessens*)

Thuringian warlord. Striped clothes like those shown here were extremely popular among the Germanic peoples. (*Photo by Sebastian Wesche-Bachmann, copyright by Lukas Handrick*)

Frankish warrior extracting his massive sword. (*Photo and copyright by Bert Tessens*)

Chapter 2

The Romano-Germanic Kingdoms, 476–613

During the central decades of the fifth century AD, Western Europe was permanently conquered by the migrating Germanic peoples and saw the formation of the Romano-Germanic kingdoms. These were new political entities with a mixed nature, since they were ruled by Germanic elites but were mostly populated by former citizens of the Western Roman Empire. The various Germanic communities that formed the new realms dominated political life thanks to their military superiority, their members being the only individuals who could bear arms. From an administrative and cultural point of view, however, the former Roman citizens preserved the functioning of their civil administrations and retained their cultural traditions. Latin continued to be the universal language of Western Europe and social life continued to be regulated by Roman law. Cultural production also remained in the hands of the former Roman citizens, who continued to have their own religious institutions. In practice, a new mixed culture was born, the result of the fusion between innovative Germanic elements brought by the newcomers and conservative Roman institutions that had existed for centuries. It is for this reason that the new realms created in Western Europe are known today as Romano-Germanic kingdoms. The encounter between the cultural superiority of Roman society and the military superiority of Germanic society gave birth to a new civilization, which shaped the history of Western Europe until the emergence of feudalism. The fusion between Germanic conquerors and Roman subjects was a complex process, which happened quite peacefully in several areas of Europe. However, there were some Germanic communities, like that of the Vandals, which refused assimilation with the Romans in order to preserve their ethnic identity. In exchange for the military protection of the newcomers, the former Roman elites of Western Europe continued to administer their territories with the efficiency that was typical of the former Empire. The system of taxation, the territorial subdivision and the religious institutions all kept working, which greatly favoured the development of new and solid national identities across Western Europe. Most of the Germanic peoples embraced the Christian faith and started to admire the immense cultural heritage left behind by the Roman Empire. During the fifth and sixth centuries, six major Germanic groups established Romano-Germanic kingdoms on the territories that had once belonged to the Roman Empire:

Frankish warrior preparing to throw his *angon* javelin. (*Photo and copyright by Bert Tessens*)

Ostrogoths, Vandals, Visigoths, Anglo-Saxons, Lombards and Franks. In addition to these, each of which will be covered in detail below, there were another eight minor Germanic communities that migrated onto former Roman lands:

Suebi: The Suebi settled in Iberia during the late fourth century, before the arrival of the Vandals. Some years later, they formed an alliance with the Romans and expelled the Vandals from modern Spain. With the subsequent arrival of the Visigoths, they were confined to a small portion of the Iberian Peninsula (in the north-west, on the territory of modern Galicia and northern Portugal). Despite being quite isolated from the rest of Europe, the Suebi repulsed several attacks of the Visigoths until being conquered by them in AD 586.

Bavarian warrior wearing his everyday clothes. (*Photo by Sebastian Wesche-Bachmann, copyright by Tobias Eisenkolb*)

Frankish warrior preparing to throw his *francisca* axe. (*Photo and copyright by Bert Tessens*)

Alamanni: The Alamanni briefly occupied a large portion of Central Europe that comprised some territories of present-day France, Germany and Switzerland. Defeated by the Franks in AD 496, they rapidly lost their independence. They tried to regain their autonomy by forming an alliance with the Ostrogoths, but this was crushed by the Franks in AD 539.

Burgundians: After being defeated by Flavius Aetius, the Burgundians occupied a portion of Gaul that was centred on the western Alps (north of Italy). They organized a kingdom that flourished for several decades until being annexed by the expanding Franks in AD 532.

Rugians: This tribe, one of the eastern Germanic communities submitted by the Huns, settled in Noricum (modern Austria) after Attila's death. With the fall of the Western Empire, they became allies of Odoacer but later joined the Ostrogoths when they invaded Italy. They were rapidly absorbed by the Ostrogoths after moving to the Italian Peninsula.

Scirii: This tribe was another of the eastern Germanic communities submitted by the Huns. After the death of Attila, they founded an independent kingdom in the former Roman province of Pannonia (modern Hungary). This realm was soon destroyed by the Ostrogoths and the few surviving Scirii joined Odoacer. When Odoacer was defeated by the Ostrogoths, the Scirii disappeared from history.

Heruli: After Attila's death, the Heruli freed themselves from Hunnic control and created their own independent kingdom in the present-day Czech Republic. Some of them supported Odoacer in Italy and were defeated by the Ostrogoths. Later, around AD 508, the realm of the Heruli was conquered and absorbed by the Lombards.

Gepids: After defeating Attila's successors and obtaining their independence, the Gepids organized a vast kingdom centred on the Carpathian Mountains. Defeated by the Ostrogoths in AD 504, they migrated southwards and settled on the territory of modern Serbia. Here they flourished for several decades, despite being defeated on several occasions by the Lombards, until being conquered by the Avars (a nomadic people of the steppes) in AD 567.

Thuringians: Settled in the central part of Germany, the Thuringians remained fully independent until AD 531/532, when they were conquered by the Franks. They later rebelled against the Franks and formed a strong alliance with the Saxons (who partly absorbed them). The Thuringians were definitively submitted by the Franks only during the reign of Charlemagne when the great king defeated the Saxons.

The Ostrogothic Kingdom

After crossing the borders of the Roman Empire, the Ostrogoths – the eastern branch of the Goths – settled in the Roman province of Dacia along the Danube. Here they prospered for some time before being submitted by the Huns, who overran

Herulian warlord wearing a *pileus pannonicus* cap made of fur. (*Photo by Sebastian Wesche-Bachmann, copyright by Rene Wissendorf Christoffersen*)

Frankish light infantryman armed with throwing javelin and throwing axe. (*Photo and copyright by Viatores*)

Thuringian light infantryman. The decorations on the tunic show a clear influence of Late Roman military fashions. (*Photo by Sebastian Wesche-Bachmann, copyright by Heiko Lipinske*)

most of Eastern Europe in a matter of a few years. As we have seen, the Ostrogoths fought against the Visigoths in Gaul as allies of Attila and were defeated together with the Hunnic leader. After the short-lived Hunnic Empire crumbled, they were permitted to settle as *foederati* in the important Roman province of Pannonia. The Ostrogoths quickly became a serious problem for the Eastern Roman Empire when they started to raid the southern Balkans from their bases in Pannonia. Eastern Emperor Zeno did not have the military resources to defeat the Ostrogoths in battle, so tried instead to transform them into allies. He offered Theodoric, the warlike king of the Ostrogoths, the possibility to settle in the Italian Peninsula as an ally of the Eastern Empire. At that time, Italy was under the control of Odoacer and his *foederati* Germanic warriors. Zeno wanted to eliminate Odoacer as soon as possible, the latter's expansionism representing a serious menace for some of his richest provinces, such as Illyricum. Trying to kill two birds with one stone, the Eastern Emperor sponsored the outbreak of a war between Theodoric and Odoacer by inviting the Ostrogoths to settle in Italy. During 476 and 488, Odoacer ruled the Italian Peninsula with great intelligence: he retained the Roman administrative system, collaborated positively with the Roman Senate as a patrician, expelled the Vandals from the rich island of Sicily and even took Dalmatia from the Eastern Empire. In the summer of 489, Theodoric invaded Italy after crossing the Julian Alps, with the promise that he would rule the Italian Peninsula as an official representative of Zeno after defeating Odoacer. Two bloody battles were fought between the Ostrogoths and the *foederati* who had settled in Italy; one took place on the banks of the Isonzo River and the other at Verona. Both clashes were won by the Ostrogoths, who nevertheless suffered heavy losses. Defeated, Odoacer fled to his capital at Ravenna, from where he continued to fight with his remaining forces. During 490, he was even able to menace – at least temporarily – the supply lines of the Ostrogoths. At this point of the war, the Visigoths who had settled in southern Gaul decided to help Theodoric in his campaign of conquest, and thus invaded Italy from the north-west. Outnumbered, Odoacer was finally defeated on 11 August 490 in a pitched battle fought on the banks of the Adda River. He fled to Ravenna, where he was besieged by Theodoric for more than two years. The Ostrogoths experienced serious difficulties in taking the former imperial capital, which was heavily fortified and could be resupplied by sea. On 25 February 493, however, Odoacer decided to come to terms with the besiegers due to the exhaustion of his troops. A peace treaty was signed, according to which Italy was divided into two parts. However, during the banquet that took place after the signing of the treaty, Theodoric assassinated Odoacer with his own hands. The defenders of Ravenna at this point had no choice but to join the Ostrogoths or be massacred by them.

After four years of harsh campaigning, Theodoric was now the master of Italy. He started to act as an independent ruler, despite preserving his formal position of an ally of the Eastern Empire. Like Odoacer, Theodoric retained the Roman administrative structures and collaborated with the Senate; he did not modify the existing laws, although these were applied only to his Roman subjects. The Ostrogoth monarch collaborated positively with the most important functionaries of the Roman administration and enjoyed good relations with the Christian Church. From a diplomatic point of view, Theodoric was a very skilled monarch. Indeed, by using marriage as a diplomatic tool, he concluded alliances with all the Germanic peoples living on the borders of Italy. When the Franks attacked the Visigoths in southern France during 506, Theodoric sided with the Franks and sent his troops into Gaul. The Ostrogoths obtained several significant victories and expanded their own territories at the expenses of the Burgundians (whose realm bordered with Italy). When the Burgundian realm was conquered by the Franks, Theodoric occupied more territories in Provence. In 504, the Ostrogoths reconquered their former homeland of Pannonia from the Gepids, which led them to fight a brief war with the Eastern Empire. Theodoric died on 30 August 526, after having transformed his realm into one of Western Europe's major powers. He was succeeded by his infant grandson, Athalric, supervised by his mother, Amalasuntha, as regent. The weakness of Theodoric's successors severely damaged the Ostrogoths' international position, especially after Athalric died at a very young age. In 534, Amalasuntha was deposed by her cousin, Theodahad, who was chosen by the Ostrogoths as their new king. After the former queen was executed in 535, Eastern Emperor Justinian invaded Italy with his victorious military forces, which, under the guidance of the great general Belisarius, had recently destroyed the Vandal Kingdom in northern Africa.

The army of Belisarius landed in Sicily in 535 and quickly captured the island, whose population had always resented Ostrogothic rule. At the same time, a Roman expeditionary force attacked the Ostrogoth positions in Dalmatia but was soundly defeated. At this point, Emperor Justinian decided to employ his best troops against the Ostrogoths, launching a successful new offensive in Dalmatia and ordering Belisarius to land on mainland southern Italy from Sicily. The great general advanced rapidly across southern Italy, aided by the weakness of the Ostrogoths in the region. The important city of Naples was besieged by the Romans for three weeks before being conquered and sacked. Belisarius then moved north against the city of Rome, which he occupied without fighting. The loss of the former imperial capital was a major blow for the reputation of Theodahad, who was deposed by his nobles and replaced as monarch by Vitiges. The new king assembled a large army and moved against Belisarius, besieging him inside Rome. The Ostrogoth siege lasted for a year,

Frankish light infantryman armed with short throwing javelins. (*Photo and copyright by Viatores*)

Thuringian light infantryman. Note the peculiar decorations of the shield.
(*Photo by Sebastian Wesche-Bachmann, copyright by Heiko Lipinske*)

only coming to an end in 538 when a Roman attack against Ariminum (present-day Rimini) obliged Vitiges to abandon Rome without having taken it. The Ostrogoths besieged Ariminum with significant military forces, but were forced to fall back on their capital of Ravenna when a new Roman contingent, commanded by the general

Alamannic archer using his wooden longbow. (*Photo by Sebastian Wesche-Bachmann, copyright by Bernd Gerstner*)

Narses, entered the Italian Peninsula. Despite the personal rivalry existing between Belisarius and Narses, the generals continued to obtain significant victories over the Ostrogoths. After the important city of Mediolanum (Milan) fell to the Romans, Vitiges decided to ask for the military help of the Franks and the Burgundians. Considering the renewed Roman military presence in Italy as a serious threat, the Franks and Burgundians responded by sending thousands of warriors across the Alps to help the Ostrogoths. Mediolanum came under siege for several months and was retaken by Vitiges, mostly because it had a small and badly supplied garrison. After the fall of this city, Emperor Justinian decided to recall Narses, leaving Belisarius as the sole supreme commander of the Roman forces in Italy. At this point of the war, something quite unexpected happened. A large Frankish army moved towards the Ostrogoths and the Romans, who were camped along the Po River. Vitiges was sure that the Franks had entered the Italian Peninsula to support him against the Romans, but when the Frankish warriors reached the Po, they suddenly attacked the Ostrogoths, who were soundly defeated and had to abandon most of northern Italy. The Franks had not attacked the Ostrogoths to support the Romans, but to conquer Italy for themselves. As a consequence, they had to face Belisarius after defeating Vitiges. However, an outbreak of dysentery in the Frankish camp soon caused thousands of deaths and forced the invaders to return north of the Alps. After these events, Belisarius received significant reinforcements and moved against the Ostrogoth capital of Ravenna. At this point, Justinian decided to put a temporary end to the hostilities since he was about to launch a large-scale invasion of the Persian Empire in the Middle East. The emperor offered a partition of Italy to Vitiges, who readily accepted such terms. The portion of the peninsula located north of the Po was to remain under Ostrogoth control, while the rest of Italy was occupied by the Romans. Nevertheless, Belisarius refused to respect the terms of the treaty and conquered Ravenna without having any official orders to do so. An informal truce then began between the two warring sides, but it did not last for long.

After Belisarius left Italy for Constantinople, the Ostrogoths started reorganizing themselves militarily. They still controlled some important cities in northern Italy, such as Pavia – which became their new capital – and Verona. The ambitious Totila was chosen as the new monarch of the Ostrogoths and started to obtain some significant successes against the Romans. Taking advantage of the ongoing Roman-Persian War and of the outbreak of the Plague of Justinian, which affected the whole of the Mediterranean region and Europe, he gained numerical superiority over the Roman troops deployed in Italy and defeated them at the Battle of Faventia. The Romans were swiftly forced to abandon both northern and central Italy, and tried to establish a defensive line in the south of the peninsula. The advance of the Ostrogoths

Ostrogoth archer wearing Phrygian cap, the distinctive headgear of Germanic archers. (*Photo by Sebastian Wesche-Bachmann, copyright by Florian Aumann*)

Herulian archer. The composite bow and quiver are identical to those used by the nomadic peoples of the steppes (such as the Huns). (*Photo by Sebastian Wesche-Bachmann, copyright by Rene Wissendorf Christoffersen*)

Herulian warrior firing with his composite bow. Note the use of a small round shield for personal protection. (*Photo by Sebastian Wesche-Bachmann, copyright by Rene Wissendorf Christoffersen*)

continued, Totila occupying most of the countryside, with only the major coastal centres – which could be resupplied by sea – remaining under Roman control. In 543, the Ostrogoths recaptured Naples and then organized a new siege of Rome. At this point of the war, Belisarius was sent back to Italy with 200 ships and a large army. The Romans reconquered most of southern Italy, but were unable to relieve Rome. The old capital's population, short of food supplies, was in a desperate situation. On 17 December 546, Totila entered Rome at the head of his victorious warriors. The city was violently plundered and had many of its walls demolished. Just four months later, however, Belisarius reoccupied Rome with his army before being recalled to

Constantinople. In 549, the Ostrogoths reconquered Rome again after most of Belisarius' troops had left Italy. As had happened before, the campaigns fought by Justinian on other fronts had a negative impact over the war against the Ostrogoths, since they absorbed much of the Romans' manpower. In 551, Narses crossed the Adriatic Sea at the head of a new army, mustering 25,000 men, most of whom were Germanic warriors, notably Lombards. After disembarking at Ancona, the Roman troops moved against the main Ostrogoth army and defeated it decisively at the Battle of Taginae. This battle was a disaster for the Ostrogoths, with Totila being killed together with the best of his military forces. Hostilities between Ostrogoths and Romans in Italy continued for another two years, but now at a lower intensity. They finally came to an end after the last forces of the Ostrogoths were crushed at the Battle of Mons Lactarius in 553. The long and bloody conflict known as the Greco-Gothic War ended with the disappearance of the Ostrogoth Kingdom and the victory of Justinian. Italy, however, emerged from the war as a depopulated and impoverished country that was open to conquest by other Germanic peoples. Indeed, later in 553 a Frankish army of some 30,000 men crossed the Alps and devastated a large portion of northern Italy, looting many cities before Narses assembled his troops in order to mount a counter-offensive. This culminated with the Battle of the Volturnus, the bloodiest clash ever fought between Franks and Romans. Narses prevailed, but only after suffering some severe losses. The Franks were not decisively defeated and continued to control several cities in the north of the Italian Peninsula. It was not until 562 that their last strongholds were subjugated. The Frankish invaders had been supported by significant numbers of Ostrogoths who had survived the Greco-Gothic War, and this did nothing but augment the devastation caused by the new conflict that took place in Italy. As we will see, soon after the end of these events, the Italian Peninsula was invaded by a new warlike Germanic community, the Lombards, who had already fought as auxiliaries of Narses against the Ostrogoths.

The Vandal Kingdom

As described above, Justinian's dream of re-annexing Italy to the Roman Empire became reality only at the end of a major military conflict that had extremely negative consequences for the Eastern Roman Empire, both politically and economically. Although the Roman reconquest of the Italian Peninsula was not to last for long, it should be remembered that Justinian's plans for the occupation of Italy were part of a larger political/military project whose main objective was retaking the territories of the former Western Empire. This ambitious project began before the Greco-Gothic War, when Justinian decided to attack the Germanic Kingdom of the Vandals in

North Africa. The Vandals were one of various Germanic communities that moved from Pannonia towards the Rhine by travelling west along the Danube during the year 405. Before entering Gaul, together with their nomadic Alan allies, they had to fight a brief but bloody conflict with the Franks who had already settled along the banks of the Rhine and were determined to protect their newly conquered homeland. The Vandals prevailed in this war thanks to the decisive military role played by the Alans, an Iranic people from the steppes of Central Asia whose military forces fought as light cavalry equipped with composite bows. After crossing the frozen Rhine, the Vandals devastated a large portion of Gaul before moving to the southern region of Aquitaine. From there they crossed the Pyrenees into the Iberian Peninsula, where some other minor Germanic peoples – including the Suebi – had already been permitted to settle by the weak authorities of the Western Roman Empire. After settling in Spain, the Vandals and the Alans experienced a series of difficulties: they were attacked from the north by the Visigoths who had settled in Septimania (southern France) and had to face strong resistance mounted by the Roman inhabitants of Iberia and the Suebi. In 422, the Vandals secured a decisive victory over the Romans and Suebi at the Battle of Tarraco, thanks to which they could stabilize their position in Spain. During the following years they developed significant naval capabilities, learning how to navigate across the Mediterranean and building a substantial fleet. The Vandals, along with the Saxons, were the only Germanic communities that became a significant naval power, starting to act as pirates by raiding several important islands and coastal cities of the Mediterranean.

Within a few years they pillaged the Balearic Islands, Carthago Spartaria (modern Cartagena) and Hispalis (modern Seville) with their seaborne attacks. In 428, the new ambitious monarch of the Vandals, Genseric, abandoned the Iberian Peninsula and moved to Roman northern Africa in order to develop a kingdom in that area of the Mediterranean. After the Vandals left Spain, the land was mostly occupied by the Suebi. In 429, Genseric led 80,000 Vandals and Alans to Roman Africa, having been invited to do so by the Roman military leader of the region, Bonifacius. Having great personal ambitions, Bonifacius wanted to become Western Roman Emperor with the help of the Vandals. However, the Vandals soon turned against him and decisively defeated his forces in battle. The surviving Roman troops were besieged by the Vandals in the major city of Hippo Regius. The siege lasted for three months and ended without success for Genseric only after most of the city's inhabitants – including Saint Augustine – had died of starvation. In 431, a large Roman expeditionary force landed in North Africa with orders to crush the Vandals, but it was swiftly destroyed by Genseric, who resumed his offensive and finally took Hippo Regius. In 435, a treaty was concluded between Genseric and the Western

Ostrogoth heavy cavalryman charging with *contus* extra-long spear.
(*Photo by Sebastian Wesche-Bachmann, copyright by Georg Ammer*)

Empire, according to which the Vandals were to control the coastline of present-day Morocco and western Algeria. In 439, however, Genseric decided to take advantage of his enemies' military weakness and invaded the rest of Roman Africa. He seized the rich city of Carthage without a fight and transformed it into the capital of his new kingdom. Inside a few years, the Vandals and the Alans had occupied all the African territories of the Western Empire, from Morocco in the west to Tunisia in the east. Part of Libya and the whole of Egypt, however, remained under the control of the Eastern Empire.

Genseric, seeking to dominate the commercial routes that crossed the Mediterranean, sent military expeditions from his naval base at Carthage against the most important islands of the Mediterranean. The Vandals soon conquered the Balearic Islands, Sardinia and Corsica, and some years later, in 468, they also invaded the rich island of Sicily. The Vandal fleet came to dominate the western Mediterranean, rivalling the larger naval forces deployed by the Eastern Empire. The Vandal Kingdom was the first Romano-Germanic realm to be officially recognized by the authorities of the Western Empire, and even came to terms with the Eastern Empire. Genseric continued his expansion by obtaining the western portion of Libya (Tripolitania), but he was determined to destroy what remained of the Western Empire. His fleet became so dominant in the Mediterranean that it became known in Old English as 'Wendelsae', or 'Sea of the Vandals'. In 455, Genseric attacked the

Ostrogoth light cavalryman armed with throwing javelin.
(*Photo by Sebastian Wesche-Bachmann, copyright by Thomas Hanke*)

The personal equipment of a late Roman heavy infantryman of Germanic origin, including a magnificent example of a crested helmet. (*Photo and copyright by Viatores*)

city of Rome and sacked it, revealing how weak the Western Empire had become. In 468, realizing that the Vandals were becoming the most serious menace to the political stability of the Mediterranean, the Western Empire and the Eastern Empire jointly organized a massive expedition against the Vandal Kingdom. This saw the participation of some 100,000 Roman soldiers, but was soundly defeated by the Vandals at the Battle of Cape Bon. From 477, political relations between the Vandals and the Eastern Empire became peaceful, mostly because the Western Empire was no longer in existence. Inside their kingdom, however, the Vandals started to experience some significant problems, mostly caused by religious differences. Most of the Roman inhabitants of the Vandal Kingdom were Trinitarian Christians, while the Vandal elite ruling the realm comprised Arian Christians. The various Vandal monarchs who succeeded Genseric exacerbated religious tensions by marginalizing their many Trinitarian subjects and persecuting them. The Germanic elite and the Roman common population never attempted an effective form of integration. The Vandals also had to face incursions by the nomadic Berber peoples, who came from the Sahara and wished to expand northwards. Following Odoacer's conquest of Sicily, it became apparent that the Vandals were no longer the military power they had once been. In 523, Hilderic became the new ruler of the Vandals and tried to pacify his kingdom by granting religious freedom to all his subjects. After he suffered a defeat

Nice example of a spangenhelm, the standard kind of helmet worn by the Germanic warriors. (*Photo and copyright by Sebastian Wesche-Bachmann*)

Golden spangenhelm with red plume. Note the artistic quality of the decorations. (*Photo and copyright by Sebastian Wesche-Bachmann*)

while fighting against the Berbers, he was deposed in a revolt organized by the pro-Arian faction of his court.

Gelimer, cousin of Hilderic, became king and resumed the persecution of the Trinitarian Christians. These events were used as *casus belli* by Eastern Emperor Justinian, who nurtured the ambition of reconquering the Western Empire and was determined to eliminate the Vandal presence in the Mediterranean. He declared war on the Vandal Kingdom, with the intention of restoring Hilderic to the throne. In the summer of 533, a large Roman expeditionary force commanded by Belisarius landed south of Carthage with the objective of destroying the Vandal Kingdom. Belisarius soon received substantial support from the local population, which had largely retained its Roman identity and thus considered him as a liberator. The Romans advanced towards Carthage along the coastal road, in order to be supplied and supported by their superior fleet. Gelimer initially avoided a direct open field confrontation with Belisarius in order to gain some time to mobilize his army. He organized an ambush in a location known as Ad Decimum, but his plans failed badly due to a lack of coordination among his troops. After winning the Battle of Ad Decimum, Belisarius entered Carthage without encountering any further opposition. Meanwhile, Gelimer completed the mobilization of his forces and started preparing

Nice example of a spangenhelm, including an aventail on the back for protection of the neck. (*Photo and copyright by Sebastian Wesche-Bachmann*)

a counter-offensive. The Vandals approached Carthage and cut the aqueduct that supplied the city with fresh water, intending to lay siege to their former capital. Belisarius, instead of being besieged by the Vandals, decided to come out of Carthage to fight a decisive pitched battle against Gelimer. This encounter took place at Tricamarum, consisting of a cavalry clash that ended in victory for the Romans. During the pursuit that followed the battle, Belisarius took the important city of Hippo Regius and captured the Vandal royal treasure (the result of many years of naval raids conducted across the Mediterranean). Gelimer, despite having lost most of his kingdom, refused to surrender and took refuge with his last followers in the mountain stronghold of Medeus. He was blockaded by a Roman contingent for the whole winter before being forced to surrender due to lack of food. After receiving guarantees for his safety, Gelimer was sent to Carthage as a captive. The Vandal Kingdom, one of the most important Germanic realms created in the fifth century, had disappeared. The Romans re-established their presence in Africa, but had to fight for several years against the Berbers in order to pacify the rebellious tribesmen.

The Visigothic Kingdom

The Visigoths crossed the Rhine together with several other Germanic peoples and swept across Gaul, plundering and devastating any Roman settlement they encountered along the way. In AD 410, they crossed the Alps and entered Italy under the leadership of their warlike king Alaric. The Visigoths sacked Rome and looted much of the Italian Peninsula before returning to Gaul, their capture of Rome an extremely important historical event that marked the end of an era. Alaric established the main base of his power in present-day southern France, his ambition being to create a kingdom that controlled large parts of both Gaul and Iberia. The Visigoths established their capital at Toulouse and started to rule their own territories autonomously from the Western Empire. When the Huns of Attila invaded Gaul, the Visigoths sided with the Romans against the nomadic invaders and played a prominent role in the Battle of the Catalaunian Plains. During this battle, the king of the Visigoths, Theodoric, was killed. Theodoric II continued the expansionist policy of his predecessors after the Huns were expelled from Western Europe. He invaded Iberia from the north and obtained numerous significant victories over the Suebi who had settled in Spain some years before. By 466, the Visigothic Kingdom comprised most of the Iberian Peninsula and a significant portion of southern France, the Suebi having been confined to the territory of modern Galicia and northern Portugal (where they established their own realm). The Visigoths extended their control over most of southern Gaul until they came into conflict with the Franks. The Franks launched a massive attack against Visigoth territory in 507, which culminated in the Battle of Campus Vogladensis. The Visigoths were utterly defeated and their strategically important city of Toulouse was sacked by the Franks. By 508, the Visigothic Kingdom had lost all its Gallic lands except for the southern region of Septimania. The following decades saw the Visigoths concentrating their military efforts in Spain, it being impossible for them to reconquer the territories that had been recently lost in Gaul. Between 549 and 554, the Visigothic Kingdom in the Iberian Peninsula was shattered by a violent civil war, which significantly weakened its military power. Emperor Justinian, who had already destroyed the Germanic realms

Ostrogoth heavy cavalryman wearing a spangenhelm and corselet of scale armour. (*Photo by Sebastian Wesche-Bachmann, copyright by Georg Ammer*)

Ostrogoth warrior wearing a spangenhelm of the Leiden type.
(*Photo by Sebastian Wesche-Bachmann, copyright by Maximilian Streibl*)

of the Vandals and the Ostrogoths, then initiated a campaign against the Visigoths in order to reconquer Iberia for his empire. The Romans were able to occupy a strip of land located along the south-eastern coast of Spain, but their advance into Iberia was soon halted by the strong resistance of the Visigoths. A military stalemate then

Germanic round shield. (*Photo and copyright by Sebastian Wesche-Bachmann*)

began, with the Romans proving unable to conquer the interior areas of the peninsula because they depended on their fleet for supplies, while the Visigoths could not dislodge the invaders from the fortified coastal cities they controlled. In 569, the ambitious and capable Liuvigild became the new king of the Visigoths. He obtained a series of victories over the Romans and greatly reduced the portion of coastal Spain controlled by them, and also conquered and annexed the Kingdom of the Suebi to his realm.

During the following decades, the Visigothic Kingdom did not prosper, mostly due to the outbreak of civil wars that were often caused by religious differences. Nevertheless, by 624 the remaining Roman troops in southern Iberia had been

Germanic sword and round shield. (*Photo and copyright by Sebastian Wesche-Bachmann*)

defeated and expelled by the Visigoths, who also conducted several campaigns against the native peoples living in the mountains of northern Spain – the Basques and the Asturians – but without success. The Basques, in particular, continued to rule in independent tribal communities and to control some of the Pyrenees' most important mountain passes. After religious unification was achieved, the Visigothic Kingdom experienced a new period of internal stability that greatly favoured the ongoing process of nation-building. The first organic Visigothic code of laws was promulgated, the powers of the monarchy were well defined and the prerogatives of the warlike aristocrats were significantly reduced. Despite the outbreak of various sporadic civil wars, it seemed that the Visigothic Kingdom was going to develop a clear national identity, just as was happening in other areas of Europe that were dominated by Germanic peoples. In 711, however, a new menace appeared on the horizon: the Muslim Arabs. During the previous decades, the Arabs had rapidly expanded from the Middle East and conquered the whole of northern Africa from the Eastern Romans. After converting the Berber tribes to Islam, the Arabs started

Germanic *francisca* and round shield. (*Photo and copyright by Sebastian Wesche-Bachmann*)

planning an invasion of the Visigothic Kingdom from the south. In 711, taking advantage of the fact that most of the Visigoths were fighting in northern Spain against the Basques, 7,000 Muslims (mostly Berbers) landed in Iberia. These soundly defeated a Visigoth force at the Battle of Guadalete, during which the ruler of the Visigothic Kingdom, Roderic, was killed. After most of southern Spain was conquered by their troops, the Arabs sent another 18,000 men to the Iberian Peninsula during 712. These, by 716, had occupied the whole territory of the Visigothic Kingdom without having suffered any significant setbacks. Between 721 and 725, the Arabs crossed the Pyrenees and occupied the region of Septimania, the last remnant of the Visigoths' presence in southern France. In 718, an uprising of the Visigoths had taken place in Asturias, led by a nobleman named Pelagius, who was able to defeat the Muslims at the Battle of Covadonga. The Visigothic Kingdom may have disappeared, but the surviving Visigoths mixed with the native populations of northern Spain – Astures, Galicians, Cantabri and Basques – in order to form new Christian communities that continued the resistance against the Arabs. Being favoured by the mountainous nature of their home territories, the Christian resistance forces were never decisively defeated by the Muslims, thereby acting as the first embryo of the Spanish national identity that developed during the Middle Ages.

Germanic sword with a highly decorated blade. (*Photo and copyright by Bert Tessens*)

The Anglo-Saxon Kingdoms

In the early years of the fifth century, it became apparent that the Roman authorities were no longer capable of defending the vast frontiers of the western half of the Empire, since too many Germanic groups were on the move and attacking in different sectors of the border. The military resources of the Western Empire were too limited to mount an effective response to the crisis, leaving the Romans with no choice but to abandon some of their territories in order to relocate more troops along the Rhine. The political life of Roman Britannia was particularly turbulent during the late fourth and early fifth centuries, with several usurpers rebelling against the central authorities of the Empire and seceding –

albeit temporarily – from Rome. In total, five major rebellions took place in Britain during the period AD 350–410, each of which was guided by a different usurper: Magnentius (350–353), Magnus Maximus (383–388), Marcus (406), Gratian (407) and Constantine III (407). The geographical isolation of Roman Britain was one of the main factors behind the outbreak of these revolts, the central authorities of the Empire no longer having the ability to send large armies across the English Channel to crush local rebellions. On most occasions, the usurpers rising to power in Britain were capable warlords who wanted to become independent from the Empire in order to organize a better defence of their homeland from the attacks of foreign peoples like the Picts, who lived in Scotland. Rome had done very little to help the province of Britannia during the previous decades, meaning the local communities had started to feel a sense of abandonment. During the early part of the fifth century, the attacks of the Picts from the north became increasingly dangerous. Rome failed to send any reinforcements, and the leading citizens of Britannia were forced to accept the fact that they were no longer under the protection of the Empire. In AD 402, Stilicho transferred several Roman military units from Britain to the continent in order to reinforce the garrison of Gaul. Four years later, the remaining Roman military corps in Britannia revolted against the central authorities of the Empire and elected three successive 'tyrants', or usurpers: Marcus, Gratian and Constantine III. The last of these tried to become emperor and went to Gaul with some of his troops, but was comprehensively defeated in 411. As a result of these events, since 410 most of the Roman troops had left Britain and gone to Gaul. Britain had effectively ceased to be part of the Roman Empire and was now independent, even though the land remained part of the Roman cultural world. The Britons spoke Latin, were Christians and identified themselves as Romans: as a result, even if their political and military links with the Empire were severed, their civilization did not change in a dramatic way. It remained a mix of Celtic and Roman elements, which had gradually developed during the previous centuries. The laws and the economic institutions of the Britons were clearly Roman, while their material culture and religion were heavily influenced by the ancient Celtic traditions. Consequently, post-410 Britannia is commonly known as Sub-Roman Britain. The former territories of Roman Britain remained united for only a few years after the legions abandoned the island, the various local aristocrats soon starting to create small independent kingdoms based on the pre-Roman Celtic tribal identities. This fragmentation of British territory took place in a chaotic age that was characterized by many small-scale civil wars, which weakened the Britons' capability to repulse foreign invasions.

The Britons fought for several decades among themselves and against the invaders from Scotland, who over time started to include the Scots as well as the Picts. The many kings, or tyrants, who dominated Sub-Roman Britain had very few military resources at their disposal and were in no condition to counter the massive offensives organized by the Celts coming from the north. In 446, due to a general worsening of their situation, the political leaders of the former Britannia made a final appeal to the Western Empire for the Roman army to come back to their homeland. At that time, Flavius Aetius was the most important warlord of the Western Empire and it is thus probable that the appeal – commonly known as the *Gemitus Britannorum*, or 'Groans of the Britons' – was addressed to him. Flavius Aetius, however, was already experiencing serious military difficulties in countering the expansionism of Attila's Huns on the continent, and thus was in no condition to help the Britons. According to the ancient historian Gildas, in 449 – fearing a new invasion that was being organized by the Picts and the Scots – the various rulers of Britain held a council in order to find a common response to the menace represented by the Celts on their northern borders. During this important meeting, the various political leaders of Britain decided to invite some Germanic communities to their territories and to offer them food supplies in exchange for their military services. Recent combat experience had shown that the Britons were too weak to confront a large-scale invasion by the Picts and the Scots, who had formed a temporary alliance with the objective of conquering Britain. The practice of hiring Germanic warriors in exchange for various kinds of concessions was extremely common during the Late Empire, with most of the Roman army consisting of Germanic individuals who served in its ranks as mercenaries. The Germanic group chosen by the Britons was the Saxons, who were already very active in the English Channel as seaborne raiders. The Britons were well aware of the combat capabilities of the Saxons, and were confident that they would be able to defeat the alliance of the Picts and Scots.

The first ancient source mentioning the Saxons dates back to AD 356, but provides very little detail. What is known is that they entered the Rhineland during the early years of the fifth century together with several other Germanic tribes. The Saxons, thanks to the fighting ability of their warriors, were able to occupy a large part of the modern Netherlands after displacing the Franks who were already settled in that region. The Saxons also controlled the North Sea coastline of north-western Germany and the southern part of the Jutland Peninsula in present-day Denmark. As a consequence of their westwards expansion, they became one of the most prominent Germanic nations. Differently from most of the other Germanic peoples, except for the Vandals, the Saxons had significant sea-faring capabilities, using boats to conduct effective naval raids. Living in the Jutland Peninsula, they had learned how to navigate across the North Sea and had progressively improved the quality of their ships by adopting new methods of construction. Originally, the Saxons

Top-quality Germanic sword with scabbard made of white leather.
(*Photo and copyright by Sebastian Wesche-Bachmann*)

wanted to settle in the northern areas of Gaul, in present-day Belgium, but over time, it became apparent that the presence of the Franks (the strongest of all the Germani) would prevent them from expanding towards these fertile regions. With a population that was experiencing a demographic boom but was suffering from a chronic shortage of food, the Saxons had no choice but to direct their expansionist ambitions towards Britain.

In 449, the Picts launched a new devastating invasion of England and started raiding the lands located on the eastern coast of the former Britannia. By that time, a new political leader had emerged among the Britons and had assumed a prominent position. Named Vortigern, he was a local ruler who had come to control a large area of Britain. In order to stop the Pictish incursions that were destroying his realm, Vortigern sponsored the idea of forming an alliance with the Saxons. In exchange for their help against the Picts, Vortigern offered the Saxons the possibility of creating a permanent settlement in south-eastern England by assigning them some land on the Isle of Thanet. As a result of this, a first wave of Germanic warriors came to Britain under the orders of two mighty warlords, the Saxon brothers Hengest and Horsa. The first Saxons who came to Britain were not particularly numerous. They had decided

Detail of the handle of a Germanic sword. (*Photo and copyright by Sebastian Wesche-Bachmann*)

to accept the terms proposed by the Britons with the objective of simply establishing a first permanent presence in England. Within a few years, however, the number of Saxons fighting as mercenaries for the Britons increased very rapidly, and when they became enough strong the Germanic warriors started to revolt against their employers. Using as a pretext the inadequacy of their monthly supplies, the Saxons began hostilities by attacking and raiding the lands of the Britons in south-eastern England. It should be noted that only a small part of the Saxons progressively moved across the English Channel, since a sizeable number of Saxon warriors remained

Germanic sword with decorative plates of white leather in its scabbard.
(*Photo and copyright by Sebastian Wesche-Bachmann*)

Nice example of a Germanic sword. (*Photo and copyright by Sebastian Wesche-Bachmann*)

in north-western Germany and south-western Denmark throughout this period. Furthermore, the Saxons did not come to Britannia alone, being joined by another two minor Germanic groups from Denmark: the Angles and the Jutes.

In 455, after having suffered several defeats, Vortigern and his son Vortimer defeated the Saxons at the Battle of Aylesford. Horsa was killed during the clash, but the Britons' victory was not a decisive one. Indeed, the Saxons were able to obtain a major success at the Battle of Crecganford in 457. Following this setback, the Britons had no choice but to evacuate Kent, allowing the Saxons to finally permanently establish themselves on British territory. After the death of Vortimer, who had always been determined to expel the Saxons from Britain, Hengest called for a council of all the rulers of England with the promise of finding a solution to the ongoing conflict. The council, however, was a trap organized by the Saxons in order to kill the most prominent leaders of their enemies: all the Saxon warlords who attended the meeting had a knife hidden in one of their shoes and attacked the Britons during the peace conference. In what became known as the 'Treachery of the Long Knives', dozens of leading Briton aristocrats were massacred and Vortigern (together with other important leaders) was captured. Following these events, the Saxons were able to expand their territories in England very rapidly and obtained a great victory over the Britons at the Battle of Wippedesfleot in 466. For several years, being without a proper

Detail of the wooden handle of a Germanic sword.
(*Photo and copyright by Sebastian Wesche-Bachmann*)

Germanic long sword used in combination with a shorter sword having a simple handle. (*Photo and copyright by Sebastian Wesche-Bachmann*)

military leader, the Britons were obliged by the Saxons to abandon large portions of their territories. The invaders looted and pillaged without mercy, destroying with great violence all the villages that tried to resist. By 490, most of eastern and central England had already been occupied by the Saxons, who had been joined by large numbers of Angles and Jutes in their conquest of the former Britannia. At this point in the long conflict, a new leader emerged among the resisting Britons: Ambrosius Aurelianus. According to Gildas, he was a Romano-Briton aristocrat who – thanks to his military abilities – assumed command of the Britons and reorganized their resistance forces. For several years Ambrosius Aurelianus fought with great success against the invaders by using hit-and-run and scorched earth tactics, as a result of which he was able to slow down the Saxon occupation of western England.

Counting on the support of the warlike Welsh communities, who had also started to be menaced by the Saxons, Ambrosius Aurelianus was able to assemble a larger army and to fight on the open field against the Germanic invaders at the Battle of Badon Hill (AD 497). Practically nothing is known about this battle: it probably took place in Wiltshire, but even its precise dating is still uncertain. The Battle of Badon Hill, however, was a victory for Ambrosius Aurelianus and his Britons. Following this major setback for them, the Saxons temporarily halted their occupation of western England. The ancient sources do not mention Ambrosius Aurelianus in describing the events that followed the clash, meaning it is probable that the

Germanic long sword used in combination with a *seax* short sword.
(*Photo and copyright by Bert Tessens*)

Germanic sword with wooden handle, showing a clear nomadic military influence. (*Photo by Sebastian Wesche-Bachmann, copyright by Cristoph Todte*)

Germanic sword with wooden handle.
(*Photo by Sebastian Wesche-Bachmann, copyright by Lukas Handrick*)

Romano-Briton leader died soon after Badon Hill. Following the death of their great warlord, the Britons were no longer able to face the Saxons on equal terms, their political fragmentation becoming an increasingly serious problem. By 520 the Saxons controlled Kent, Sussex, East Anglia, Hampshire and Yorkshire. They started organizing their possessions as small autonomous kingdoms, while at the same time continuing to fight against the Britons in order to expand their territories. In 535 and 536, the whole of Britain experienced extreme weather that caused a major famine. This seriously affected western England and Wales – which were still under control of the Britons – and was followed by a great plague in 549. The Saxons took advantage of their enemies' difficulties to continue their conquest of England, obtaining more victories in clashes such as the Battle of Bedcanford (AD 571). The successes of the invaders, however, did not prevent the Britons from fighting against each other, with several minor civil wars breaking out. In 577, the Saxons obtained another great victory at the Battle of Dyrham, after which they were able to complete their conquest of Wessex. This clash marked a real turning point in the long war fought between the Britons and the Saxons, since it enabled the Germanic invaders to overrun the salient still controlled by the Britons around the London area and to annex the Midlands to their territorial possessions. With the occupation of Watling Street and Bath, the Saxons could finally separate the Britons living in Wales from those who were still free in south-western England.

During the second half of the sixth century, the Angles and the Jutes were also particularly active in settling more lands taken from the Britons. While the Angles moved north along the coastline of eastern England, the Jutes became predominant in Kent. In AD 590, several Briton kings formed a military alliance in the hope of stopping the Saxons in Wiltshire, as Ambrosius Aurelianus had done almost a century before. Against all odds, they defeated the Germanic invaders at the Battle of Woden's Burg in 592, thereby gaining more time to reorganize their defences. While these events took place in the west, in the east the Angles continued their expansion across Northumbria and landed a large invading force on the Fife coast in south-eastern Scotland in 596. The Picts and the Scots, who had been at war with the Britons for many decades, understood that the Germanic warriors represented a deadly menace for them and thus joined forces with the Britons, forming a temporary military alliance. This, however, was soon defeated by the Angles at the Battle of Raith. Thereafter, the Britons' presence in north-eastern England became weaker and the alliance between the Picts and the Scots came to an abrupt end. In 597, Pope Gregory I sent Saint Augustine of Canterbury to Kent, with orders to convert to Christianity the Germani living in Britain. By the year 600, almost the whole territory of present-day England had been conquered by the Saxons, Angles and

Jutes, with only some small areas of north-western England remaining independent from the Germanic invaders. The Angles progressively extended their dominance over the north-eastern lands of East Anglia, Mercia and Northumbria, whereas the Jutes replaced the Saxons in Kent and established themselves on the Isle of Wight and in some areas of Hampshire. Militarily, the Saxons were much stronger than the Angles and the Jutes, being both more numerous and more warlike. Saxon territorial possessions in England gradually started to be organized as four autonomous realms: the Kingdom of the East Saxons or (Kingdom of Essex), the Kingdom of the Middle Saxons (Kingdom of Middlesex), the Kingdom of the South Saxons (Kingdom of Sussex) and the Kingdom of the West Saxons (Kingdom of Wessex). These new Saxon kingdoms soon started to fight against each other for dominance over all of England. Over time, seven states emerged from the conflicts that ravaged southern Britain and a new political system was established. This, known as the Heptarchy due to the number of kingdoms it comprised, was relatively stable and continued to exist until the arrival of the Vikings decisively altered the balance of power in England. The seven kingdoms that made up the Heptarchy were Wessex, Essex, Sussex, Mercia, East Anglia, Northumbria and Kent. The first four were inhabited by the Saxons, East Anglia and Northumbria by the Angles and Kent by the Jutes. It should be noted that until the ascendancy of Alfred the Great during the Viking era, the states making up the Heptarchy were not the only ones existing in England, several sub-kingdoms having been formed. These were usually client states of the major realms, but sometimes – for short periods of time – acted as autonomous political entities.

The Lombard Kingdom

The Lombards were one of the last Germanic peoples to enter the territory of the Roman Empire in the Danubian sector. According to contemporary chronicles, they were more wild and warlike than the other Germani as they had experienced very little contact with the sophisticated civilization of the Roman world. During the early part of the sixth century, the Lombards fought in Pannonia against the Gepids, who had settled there some years before. After several harshly fought military campaigns, they gradually prevailed, partly thanks to support provided by Emperor Justinian. By 551, the Lombards had acquired complete control over the strategic region of Pannonia and were trusted allies of the Eastern Romans. As we have seen, during the last phase of the Greco-Gothic War they also provided various strong contingents of auxiliaries to the general Narses. In 560, the ambitious Alboin became the new king of the Lombards during a period of great political changes for most of Europe. In 567, Alboin completely destroyed what remained of the Gepids after forming a strong military alliance with the nomadic Avars. He then started considering the possibility of invading Italy in order to exploit the military weakness of the Eastern Romans in the Italian Peninsula after the end of the Greco-Gothic War. In the spring of 568, fearing that the aggressive Avars could now turn on his people, Alboin migrated with his Lombards from Pannonia to Italy. The first major city to be conquered by the Lombards was Forum Iulii (present-day Cividale del Friuli), which soon became the main operational base of Alboin's forces due to its strategic position. In the summer of 569, the Lombards conquered the large city of Mediolanum and continued their spectacular advance, aided by the weakness of the Eastern Roman forces that they encountered. Pavia, which later became the capital of the new Lombard Kingdom, was then besieged for three years by the Lombards until it fell in 572. During the following years most of northern Italy was occupied by the newcomers, except for some coastal centres that could be resupplied by sea from Constantinople. The Lombards then penetrated into central and southern Italy, establishing two new and semi-autonomous territorial entities: the Duchy of Spoleto in central Italy and the Duchy of Benevento in southern Italy. These duchies were initially placed under the direct control of the Lombard Kingdom in the north, but over time they became largely autonomous. By the end of this first phase of Lombard conquest, the Eastern Romans retained possession only of Ravenna and Rome in northern-central Italy, the cities linked by a thin Roman-controlled corridor that ran through the urban settlement of Perugia.

The Lombard Kingdom never had a strong monarchy, its central government always having to tolerate the secessionist ambitions of the various nobles who ruled the conquered territory as *duces*, or 'dukes'. Each of these dukes pursued his own political interests by ruling autonomously and plotted to become king. This unstable political situation led to the final collapse of the Roman administrative structure, partly because the Lombards – at least initially – seemed to have no interest in mixing with the local population of Italy. In 584, Autari became the new king of the Lombards, marking the beginning of a new historical phase in the history of the kingdom. He reinforced the military structures of his kingdom to limit the expansionism of the Franks in north-western Italy, while also forming a strong alliance with the Bavarii, a Germanic community that had settled in present-day Bavaria and represented a significant regional power. During the early years of the seventh century, under the guidance of their new monarch, Agilulf, the Lombards conquered several important areas of northern Italy that had remained under control of the Eastern Romans (who, after Justinian's death, should more correctly be called Byzantines). The semi-autonomous southern duchies of Spoleto and Benevento also expanded at the expense

Germanic sword and *seax*. (*Photo by Sebastian Wesche-Bachmann, copyright by Tobias Eisenkolb*)

of the Byzantines, assuming a more solid political structure. A new system of royal officials was created to administer the various territories of the Lombard Kingdom more effectively. At the same time, a new process of cultural integration was initiated, which led to the progressive conversion of the Lombards – who were mostly pagans or Arians – to Catholicism. The Lombard kings developed positive relations with the papacy ruling the city of Rome – which became increasingly autonomous from Byzantine control – and established many rich monasteries throughout the Italian

Germanic thrusting axe carried with a sword and knife.
(*Photo by Sebastian Wesche-Bachmann, copyright by Cristoph Todte*)

Peninsula. After the death of Agilulf in 616, a civil war broke out in the Lombard Kingdom that led to the rise of a new royal family. This was made up of Arians and was opposed to the process of cultural pacification that was taking place in Italy. The aggressive Rothari ruled as monarch of the Lombards from 636–652, conducting several military campaigns against the Byzantines that led to their final expulsion from most of northern Italy. Rothari obliged the dukes of Spoleto and Benevento to recognize his superior authority, and also codified in a written form the rules and customs of his own people by enacting an important edict (the famous Edict

Detail of the belt equipment used to carry a sword and short knife. (*Photo and copyright by Sebastian Wesche-Bachmann*)

Detail showing the belt equipment needed to carry a sword and *seax*.
(*Photo and copyright by Martin Just*)

of Rothari). After Rothari's death, the Lombard Kingdom entered a new phase of internal conflict, which saw a progressive weakening of the central government. In addition, the relations of the Lombards with the papacy worsened, while the Franks started to make their presence felt again on the north-western borders of Italy.

During this new historical phase, the political life of the Lombard Kingdom started to be dominated by the clash between two opposing factions: one was favourable to the 'romanization' of the Lombards' customs, while the other wanted to preserve the original Germanic identity of its people. With the ascendancy to the throne of

Nice example of a Germanic waist-belt. Note the practice of having a short knife inside the small leather bag. (*Photo by Sebastian Wesche-Bachmann, copyright by Maximilian Streibl*)

Liutprand in the early eighth century, the Lombard Kingdom was reunified and temporarily pacified. The new monarch, who reigned for more than thirty years, formed an important alliance with the Franks and restored positive relations with the papacy. Liutprand presented himself as the defender of Catholicism and joined the Roman Church in an anti-Byzantine coalition. He defeated the Byzantines on several occasions and significantly reduced their presence on Italian territory. To seal his alliance with the papacy, Liutprand donated Rome and most of the city's surroundings to the church; this transformed the Roman Church into a proper political entity with its own independent territory. Under Liutprand's rule, the Lombard Kingdom

Germanic *seax* short sword. (*Photo by Sebastian Wesche-Bachmann, copyright by Stephan Becker*)

stabilized. The offices of the central government were completely reorganized in order to become more efficient, new laws were promulgated, commerce flourished and the various social groups started to co-exist peacefully. The last great monarch of the Lombards was Aistulf, who achieved several notable military successes, including the conquest of Ravenna in 751. His expansionist moves, however, terrorized the papacy into forming a military alliance with the powerful Franks. The Franks, who had long nurtured ambitions of conquering Italy, launched an invasion of the Italian Peninsula in 754 under the leadership of Pepin the Short (father of Charlemagne). Aistulf was soundly defeated by the Franks and was made to accept humiliating peace terms: he had to cede Ravenna and the surrounding territories to the Roman Church, in addition to paying substantial compensation to the Franks. After Aistulf's death, the Lombard Kingdom came under the leadership of Desiderius, a clever and discreet politician who organized the marriage of his daughter, Desiderata, to the son of Pepin the Short, Charlemagne. With this political move, Desiderius hoped to preserve his realm's independence.

The Frankish Kingdom

The Franks appeared on the borders of the Roman Empire around AD 280, when they started to launch devastating incursions along the Rhine. After suffering early defeats, they began living on the borders of Roman territories as 'land pirates' and experienced a demographic boom. During the 350s, the Franks started to be described by contemporary Roman chroniclers as consisting of two autonomous communities: the Salians and the Ripuarians. The Salians progressively settled over an area of north-eastern Gaul that became known as Neustria, while the Ripuarians established themselves in an area of north-western Germania that became known as Austrasia. The territories of the Salians and the Ripuarians had a long border in common, which was the scene of several conflicts fought between the two main communities of the Franks. With the fall of the Western Roman Empire in 476, the role played by the Franks in Gaul became extremely important. It should be remembered, however, that a large part of present-day France was still under the control of a powerful Roman warlord named Syagrius. During a period of great political chaos, Syagrius had carved out for himself a private realm in northern Gaul and had been able to defend it from the expansionism of the Germanic peoples living on its borders: the Visigoths in the south-west, the Burgundians in the south-east, the Salian Franks in the north-west and the Ripuarian Franks in the north-east. Syagrius was the son of the last Roman overall military commander of Gaul, inheriting from his father control over a vast territory located between the Somme and the Loire rivers that had as its capital the city of Soissons. Syagrius, despite being isolated from the rest of the Western Empire, managed to rule his realm as an independent Gallo-Roman enclave until the ascendancy of Clovis as the new leader of the Salian Franks in 481. Clovis was the founder of the Franks' military power, unifying the Salian and Ripuarian Franks under his guidance before invading the part of Gaul that was controlled by Syagrius. The decisive clash between the Gallo-Romans and the Franks took place in 486 at Soissons and ended with a great victory for Clovis, who crushed his opponents and then conquered all the Gallo-Roman territory. Thanks to their success at the Battle of Soissons, the newly unified Franks could double in size the area of northern Gaul that was under their dominance. In the 490s, Clovis and his Franks had to fight several wars against other Germanic communities that wanted to settle in Gaul: the Burgundians, the Thuringians and the Alamanni. The clash with the Alamanni was particularly harsh, due in the main to them being a historical enemy of the Ripuarian Franks. The decisive battle between Franks and Alamanni took place at Tolbiac in 496. The Franks came very near to complete defeat, but were eventually able to prevail. Clovis attributed his victory to a vow he had made during the battle that he would convert to the religion of the Christian God if he helped him. As a result, after

Germanic *seax* with a highly decorated leather scabbard. (*Photo and copyright by Bert Tessens*)

The personal equipment of a Germanic warrior, including sword and point of the spear. (*Photo and copyright by Sebastian Wesche-Bachmann*)

Germanic *francisca* throwing axe. (*Photo and copyright by Bert Tessens*)

Detail of the head of a *francisca* axe. (*Photo and copyright by Viatores*)

victory, he was baptized at Reims – the capital of the Franks – on Christmas Day 496. This event was of great historical importance, as after their victory at Tolbiac the Franks and their monarchs became the strongest defenders of Catholicism among the kingdoms of Germanic Europe. The Alamanni, defeated, abandoned the lands they had previously inhabited, which freed the Ripuarian Franks from a powerful potential threat. Thereafter, the union between the Salians and Ripuarians became permanent.

After defeating the Alamanni, Clovis turned his attention to the Burgundians and – more importantly – to the Visigoths, who had come to control a large part of central Gaul. New inter-Germanic wars were going to decide if the territory of present-day France would be ruled by the Franks or the Visigoths. During 500 and 501, Clovis intervened in the civil war that ravaged the realm of the Burgundians, hoping to obtain fresh territories. At the end of the hostilities, despite not having been able to crush the Burgundians, he secured tribute from them. The Visigoths had been trying to make the Burgundians their vassals for a long time, so the events of 500–501 resulted in a worsening of relations between the Franks and Visigoths. In 507, Clovis launched a massive invasion of the Visigothic lands in Aquitaine, seeking to gain a decisive victory that would give him dominance over most of Gaul. The final clash between Franks and Visigoths took place at the Battle of Vouillé in 507, which was an extremely bloody affair. Clovis eventually managed to crush the Visigoths of Alaric, who died during the clash, significantly weakening the military power of his people. After their victory, the Franks swiftly occupied the Visigoth capital of Toulouse, seizing control of most of southern Gaul except for the region of Septimania. During 507 and 508, the Visigoths tried to conduct a counter-offensive, but this was repulsed by Clovis. The king died in 511, having ruled the Franks during

Leather quiver used by the eastern Germanic peoples. The nomadic military influence is very clear in its shape. (*Photo by Sebastian Wesche-Bachmann, copyright by Bernd Gerstner*)

an age of great battles and conquests. He left behind a unified Frankish Kingdom that comprised most of Gaul and areas of western Germania. The Franks, thanks to the victories of Clovis, were now the leading military power among the Romano-Germanic realms of Europe. Clovis is today considered by most historians as the true

Decorated buckle of a Germanic waist-belt.
(*Photo by Sebastian Wesche-Bachmann, copyright by Tobias Eisenkolb*)

Buckle of a Germanic waist-belt. (*Photo and copyright by Sebastian Wesche-Bachmann*)

founder of the nation that later became known as France. He was the creator of a new dynasty, known as the Merovingians from the name of a mythical Salian monarch, Merovech, who – according to legend – had ruled during the time of Attila's invasion of Gaul. After Clovis' death, the new Merovingian dynasty experienced serious problems, the Frankish Kingdom having been divided among the former king's sons according to the contemporary Germanic practice. Each realm was considered to be the private property of the king, and as such had to be divided among his direct male heirs. Each succession usually produced great political fragmentation and the outbreak of civil wars, which is exactly what happened in Gaul following Clovis' death. After a period of bloody civil conflicts, the Frankish Kingdom was briefly reunified in 613, but this did not last for long. During the seventh century, four autonomous Frankish political entities emerged in Gaul (each of which was ruled by a branch of the Merovingians): Austrasia, Neustria, Burgundy and Aquitaine.

Detail showing the metal components of a late Roman waist-belt used by Germanic warriors. (*Photo and copyright by Viatores*)

These realms corresponded to previous territorial subdivisions, which existed before Clovis' unification of the Franks and before the victories of the Franks over both the Burgundians and the Visigoths. The divisions existing among the Merovingians favoured the ascendancy of their warlike nobility, whose members delighted in being ruled by weak monarchs.

Chapter 3

The Ascendancy of the Carolingians, 613–768

From 613, the political life of the Merovingian territories started to be dominated by a powerful and ambitious noble family, the Pippinids, who rose to prominence quite rapidly thanks to the military capabilities of its members. Their name derived from that of the first important member of the warlike clan, Pippin I. Taking advantage of the Merovingian monarchs' weakness, the Pippinids became the real power behind the throne, despite the opposition of the rival family of the Arnulfings. They obtained for themselves the important position of mayors of the palace, mediating between the monarch and all the magnates of the kingdom. The mayor of the palace was the most important non-royal person in the Frankish realms. The political office was created in 613 and started to be controlled by the Pippinids from 624. For decades, the Pippinids acted as kingmakers in Austrasia, organizing coups and political assassinations that were all aimed at transforming the ruling monarchs into their own puppet kings. The various mayors of the palace all worked hard to form a strong alliance with the church, in the hope that their clan would eventually be in the position to replace the declining Merovingian royal family. The seventh century was a chaotic period for the Frankish lands, with the outbreak of several civil wars – usually a clash between Pippinids and Arnulfings – as well as various conflicts that were fought between Austrasia and Neustria. The Kingdom of Neustria also had its mayors of the palace, who controlled the political life of their kingdom and whose ambition was to remove the weak members of the Merovingian family. In 639, the rivalry between the Pippinids and Arnulfings came to an end when two important members of the noble families were married. This union gave birth to Pippin of Héristal, also known as Pippin II, who was to become a key figure in the history of Western Europe. During the late seventh century, Pippin II, as mayor of the palace of Austrasia, obtained a series of key military victories and was able to expand his political influence over Neustria, where he also became mayor of the palace.

Pippin II was the first Frankish leader for many years to look outside the borders of his country, conducting expansionist campaigns in Frisia (present-day Netherlands) as well as in western Germany. When he died in 714, the Pippinids had complete control over the political life of both Austrasia and Neustria. The Merovingian kings

Carolingian warlord wearing a sallet helmet (a conical open-faced helmet, offering a high degree of visibility, developed during the early Carolingian period and probably derived from Late Roman helmets) and a full set of scale armour. (*Photo by Julien Souris, copyright by Gisna Missi Dominici*)

Carolingian heavy cavalryman equipped with a complete set of scale armour. (*Photo by Julien Souris, copyright by Gisna Missi Dominici*)

could take no decisions without the consent of Pippin II, their status having been reduced to that of mere symbolic figures. Following Pippin II's death, the Neustrians rebelled against the Pippinids and allied themselves with the Frisians, assembling a large army to invade Austrasia. It was during this period of chaos that a great warlord emerged among the Pippinids to become the new leader of the family: Charles Martel. An illegitimate son of Pippin II, he became known as 'Martel', or 'Little Mars', only after obtaining a series of brilliant military victories. Despite being quite young, Charles was able to defeat the Neustrian invasion of Austrasia, and by 720 he was mayor of the palace of both Austrasia and Neustria, just like his father. In just a few years, Charles Martel became the most powerful military leader of Western Europe, to the point that his family – which was the result of the union between the Pippinids and Arnulfings – assumed the new collective denomination of Carolingians. The political instability that had characterized the period following Pippin II's death had greatly damaged the interests of the Franks; both Aquitaine and Burgundy, for example, had slipped from Frankish control. In addition, the Saxons had taken advantage of the Merovingian weakness to expand their territories at the expense of the Franks. Charles Martel fought against the Saxons from 720–724 and was able to secure the northern borders of Austrasia and Neustria, and reimposed the political control of his family over the minor Frankish realms of Aquitaine and Burgundy. Charles also invaded the territory of the Alamanni, who had been tributaries of the Franks since the time of Clovis but who had rebelled following Pippin II's death. The capable mayor of the palace created a very strong alliance with the papacy, establishing several pro-Carolingian episcopal centres on Frankish territory as well as building many abbeys.

In 725, moving from Alamannia, Charles Martel invaded Bavaria, which until then had been a semi-autonomous kingdom ruled by a Frankish royal family – the Agilolfings – since 548. Bavaria, at least on paper, was a vassal state of the Merovingians. However, its rulers had started to develop an independent foreign policy and had formed a strong alliance with the Lombard Kingdom of Italy. Charles restored the Merovingians' predominance over Bavaria and started to nurture the ambition of conquering the Italian Peninsula. In 731, however, the Arabs of Spain crossed the Pyrenees to invade Frankish Aquitaine, causing a military emergency as the Muslims advanced rapidly towards the Loire River after destroying all the local forces they encountered along the way. In 721, the Franks of Aquitaine had already repelled an Arab incursion, but this time the Muslim invasion force was much larger. The Muslims devastated a large portion of southern Gaul before Charles Martel could mobilize his troops and move against them. The decisive clash between Franks and Arabs took place in 732 at the Battle of Poitiers. Charles Martel commanded a strong infantry force mostly made up of veteran soldiers, while his Muslim opponents could count on numerically superior cavalry forces. The Muslim cavalry charged repeatedly against the Frankish positions, but each time were repulsed by Charles' disciplined infantrymen. Charles Martel obtained a fundamental victory for Christian Europe, forcing the Arabs to return south of the Pyrenees. This success transformed the Carolingians into the defenders of Catholicism, which had great symbolic importance. Nevertheless, the threat posed by the Muslims did not vanish. Indeed, the Arabs invaded Gaul again in 735, looting Arles and remaining in present-day southern France for several years. Charles responded by organizing an effective counter-offensive, but he was unable to expel the Muslims from the region of Septimania, which they had conquered several years before. Charles Martel, one of the greatest military leaders of Germanic Europe, died in 741. Learning from his father, he had made secure succession plans and his extensive lands were divided between his two sons, Carloman and Pepin. Carloman became mayor of the palace in Austrasia and was also assigned both Alamannia and Thuringia, while Pepin was mayor of the palace in Neustria and also received Burgundy and Aquitaine.

The brothers quarrelled, however, and in 747 Pepin – who became known as Pepin the Short because of his stature – forced Carloman to enter a monastery and cede all his territories to him. Consequently, Pepin started to act as the sole rule of the Frankish lands (now collectively known as Francia). In 751, with the decisive support of the papacy, the Carolingians finally decided to depose the last Merovingian monarch, Childeric III, and to confine him to a monastery. Pepin was then elected King of the Franks by an assembly of Frankish nobles, receiving a papal blessing. It was the beginning of a new era for Western Europe, the new royal family of the Carolingians having ambitions to become the ruling power of the Christian world. In exchange for papal support, which was decisive in 'legalizing' his deposition of the Merovingians, Pepin accepted becoming the official defender of the church and thus put his troops at the Pope's orders when needed for protection. The first important act of the new monarch was to wage war on the Lombard Kingdom, in order to defend the papal territories from the expansionism of Aistulf, the Lombard monarch. The Franks reconquered several areas of Italy that had been lost by the papacy and donated them to the church. In 752, having defeated the Lombards, Pepin turned his attention to the Arab positions in Septimania. He organized a large expedition that lasted for several years until the main Muslim stronghold north of the Pyrenees – the city of Narbonne – was occupied by the Franks in 759. One year later, the Carolingian monarch ravaged with fire most of Aquitaine, which had remained largely independent from his family's rule since Charles Martel's death. The campaign in southern Gaul was particularly harsh, the Gascons – who were

Carolingian heavy infantryman wearing a helmet with aventail of chainmail and scale armour. (*Photo by Julien Souris, copyright by Gisna Missi Dominici*)

Carolingian warlord equipped with a helmet having an aventail of chainmail, scale armour and leather vambraces. (*Photo and copyright by Thomas Gunter*)

cousins of the Basques living in Spain – having allied themselves with Aquitaine. By 768, after having terrorized most of southern Gaul with his troops, Pepin the Short finally annexed the whole of Aquitaine to his domains, but he died unexpectedly soon after these events.

In 768, following the death of Pepin the Short, the Frankish Kingdom was divided between his two sons, according to the principles of Salic Law. The first son, Charles, was assigned Aquitaine, the northern portion of Neustria, northern Austrasia and Bavaria, while the second son, Carloman, received Burgundy, the southern part of Neustria and southern Austrasia. In practice, Charles had been assigned the poorest lands bordering with foreign territories, while Carloman was given the richer interior areas, although it should be noted that Carloman's realm was completely surrounded by Charles' dominions (which formed the shape of an arch). Charles and Carloman disliked each other, both having ambitions to reign over a unified Frankish Kingdom.

Carolingian heavy infantryman armed with spear and shield. (*Photo by Julien Souris, copyright by Les Cerfs*)

Carolingian elite warrior of the Royal Guard. (*Photo by Julien Souris, copyright by Gisna Missi Dominici*)

Tensions started to grow between the two Frankish monarchs soon after the death of their father, when the region of Aquitaine revolted against Carolingian rule. Charles and Carloman both sent armies against the rebels, but instead of supressing the uprising, the Frankish soldiers began quarrelling among themselves. The situation escalated and came very near to the outbreak of a civil war. Eventually, however, Carloman decided to return to his dominions due to the military superiority of his brother. Charles then quickly and mercilessly crushed the rebellion in Aquitaine, showing to the Frankish world that he was much more capable as a monarch than Carloman. In 770, Bertrada, the mother of two brothers who sided with Charles, launched a diplomatic offensive aimed at weakening Carloman and surrounding his lands. She arranged the marriage of Charles to Desiderata, the daughter of Lombard monarch Desiderius, in order to have a strong ally on the southern borders of Carloman's kingdom. Bertrada also established positive relations with the branch of the Carolingian family that had control over Bavaria and manoeuvred to obtain the decisive moral support of the papacy. On 4 December 771, before a full-scale war could break out between the two Frankish realms, Carloman suddenly died. Several contemporary observers accused Charles and Bertrada of having poisoned him, but according to recent investigations it seems that Carloman's death was due to natural causes. Whatever the truth, Charles was able to reunify the Frankish domains under his sole rule soon after the death of his brother. A warlike and ambitious monarch was now going to become the master of Europe.

Chapter 4

The Wars of Charlemagne, 768–814

When Charles became King of the Franks, Carolingian territory was surrounded by a series of hostile nations that were ready to wage war on the Frankish lands. In the south-west there were the Arabs of the Iberian Peninsula, who were at war with the Christian communities that had survived in northern Spain following the fall of the Visigothic Kingdom. These, since 718, had formed an autonomous realm known as the Kingdom of Asturias, which, under guidance of the warlike Pelagius (a Visigoth nobleman), had obtained a clear victory over the Muslims at the Battle of Covadonga in 722. The Kingdom of Asturias controlled a small portion of northern Spain, but it was impossible for the Arabs to conquer due to the mountainous nature of its territory. It continued to exist after the death of Pelagius in 737, renewing its struggle for survival against the Muslims. In addition to the Kingdom of Asturias, there were also various other Christian lands in northern Spain that had not been submitted by the Arabs; these were inhabited by the Basques, who lived autonomously across the Pyrenees Mountains and had strong cultural links with the Gascons of Aquitaine. The Basques loved their freedom and hated the Muslims as much as they hated the Carolingians (who were Christians like them, but had harshly submitted the Gascons). The Basques controlled the mountain passes of the Pyrenees and all the land routes connecting the Frankish lands with those of the Kingdom of Asturias. In the south-east of the Frankish Kingdom there was the Lombard Kingdom, the last surviving Romano-Germanic realm of continental Europe. The Lombard Kingdom was no longer as powerful as it had been during the previous century, no longer having direct control over the Lombard duchies of central and southern Italy. In addition, the Roman Church had created its own state in central Italy and this separated the Lombard lands of the north from those in the south. In southern Italy, there was still a significant presence of the Byzantines, who also controlled the major islands of Sicily and Sardinia thanks to their superior fleet. In the west, the Carolingian lands bordered with Brittany, the only portion of Gaul that had never been submitted by the Franks. Brittany was inhabited by independent communities of Celtic stock – the Bretons – who had a lot in common with their cousins in the British Isles (the Britons). The Bretons were extremely jealous of their independence and could count on the support of the British Celtic communities

Carolingian heavy cavalryman wearing corselet of scale armour (*brunia*).
(*Photo by Julien Souris, copyright by Les Cerfs*)

Carolingian heavy infantryman equipped with spear and shield. (*Photo and copyright by De vita aetate carolingorum*)

living in Cornwall and Wales. In the north, the Frankish domains bordered with Denmark, where the Viking culture was already developing and where paganism was still dominant. On the north-eastern frontier, the Carolingians faced their harshest enemies, the Saxons and the Thuringians. These were not organized into proper kingdoms and had retained their traditional lifestyle, which included paganism and was based on tribal social structures. The Saxon lands comprised much of present-day western Germany, while the Thuringian territory was located north of Bavaria. The Bavarians, as we have seen, were ruled by a Carolingian dynasty but enjoyed a high degree of political autonomy, being organized as a duchy. This bordered with Slavic territories in the north and the south, sharing its northern frontiers with the Bohemians/Moravians and its southern frontiers with the Slovenes/Croats. Not far from Bavaria and Italy, on the territory of present-day Hungary, were the settlements of the warlike Avars, who had come from the Eurasian steppes. These militarily powerful nomads had submitted most of the Slavic communities living around their lands. As is made clear by the above general description, Charles' reign was set to be dominated by warfare because of the existing political situation in continental Europe around the Frankish Kingdom. Indeed, he would spend most of his life as a king fighting against different enemies, in every corner of his domains.

In 772, Pope Adrian I demanded that the Lombards return various northern Italian cities that had been occupied by them some years before. Desiderius, quite unexpectedly, responded by invading the church's lands and marching on Rome. Prior to this, personal relations between Charles and Desiderius had already deteriorated, Charles having repudiated (a medieval form of divorce) his Lombard wife, Desiderata. When Adrian I officially requested Frankish military help against the Lombards, Charles crossed the Alps at the head of a massive army and rapidly chased Desiderius back to his capital of Pavia. Here, from 773–774, the surviving Lombard forces were besieged by the Franks. The siege operations were extremely difficult for Charles, the area surrounding Pavia being covered with inhospitable marshes notorious for the spreading of diseases and where there was very little clean water. While Desiderius was under siege, his son and designated successor, Adelchis, tried to raise a new army in Verona. The rapid intervention of the Franks, however, forced him to abandon his plans and flee into exile to Constantinople. In the summer of 774, having concluded a new alliance with the papacy and assigned more lands in central Italy to the Catholic Church, Charles finally took the city of Pavia. This marked the end of the Lombards' resistance: the Carolingian monarch had himself crowned with the Iron Crown of the Lombard kings and made the Lombard magnates pay homage to him in Pavia. The whole of northern Italy had been annexed to the Carolingians, a state of affairs that had seemed unthinkable just a few years before. In 776, both the Duchy of Spoleto and the Duchy of Benevento revolted against Charles' rule, which they had never recognized as legitimate since they were autonomous from the Lombard Kingdom of Desiderius. The Franks swiftly crushed the uprising and forced the Duchy of Spoleto to submit, but the Duchy of Benevento remained independent. During the following decades, Charles conducted several minor campaigns against the Lombards in the south of Italy, but despite obtaining some local victories he was never able to annex the Duchy of Benevento to his Italian domains.

From 778, Carolingian armies were heavily involved in fighting against the Muslims in the Iberian Peninsula. Charles, wishing to present himself as the champion of the Christians, nurtured ambitions of freeing Europe from the threat of the Arabs in Spain (commonly known as Moors). In 778, two large Frankish armies moved across the Pyrenees to invade the northern Moorish lands of the Iberian Peninsula. The armies met at Saragossa, where Charles received the homage of those Muslim rulers who preferred to submit rather than fight against him. The Frankish siege of Saragossa, however, ended in failure, Charles having come up against unexpectedly strong resistance. Being menaced by the arrival of a large Moorish army from the south, and with his lines of communication being over-stretched, the Carolingian monarch chose to halt his campaign to liberate the Iberian Peninsula and to return north. Here, the Franks had acquired firm control of the region of Catalonia, but had not completely subdued the Basques. Following the Frankish occupation of Pamplona, the Basques had formally subdued to Charles, but they were just waiting for the right opportunity to rise up in revolt. The Basques were masters in mountain warfare and planning ambushes, all their warriors being equipped as light infantrymen in order to conduct guerrilla operations. Armed with short spears/javelins or a longbow, each Basque fighter was capable of killing a heavily armoured Frankish warrior from long range. When Charles abandoned the siege of Saragossa and retreated north, the Basques took the opportunity to ambush the rearguard of his army while it was crossing the mountain pass of Roncesvalles in the Pyrenees. The ensuing Battle of Roncesvalles, which was more a skirmish than a proper battle, is still remembered today as one of the most famous clashes of the times. The historical events of the ambush later gave birth to *The Song of Roland*, which is regarded as the first major work of medieval French literature. In reality, the clash was a defeat for the Carolingians, whose rearguard was decimated by the Basque mountain fighters, but not a catastrophic one because most of the Frankish army was able to successfully cross the Pyrenees to safety. The Spanish campaign had been the first significant failure in the military career of Charles.

Nevertheless, Charles continued to fight against the Moors and the Basques for most of his life. In 785, the Franks captured the city of Girona and consolidated

Carolingian standard-bearer wearing a corselet of scale armour. (*Photo by Julien Souris, copyright by Gisna Missi Dominici*)

Carolingian warlord (left), junior aristocrat (centre) and heavy cavalryman (right). Note the excellent manufacture of the scale armour worn by two of the figures. (*Photo by Julien Souris, copyright by Gisna Missi Dominici*)

their control over the Spanish region of Catalonia, which had not been abandoned after the unsuccessful campaign of 778. In 795, the Carolingian domains south of the Pyrenees were organized as the Hispanic March, a border territory that also comprised Septimania and existed in a state of continuous war with the Muslims. In 797, Barcelona, the largest city of Catalonia, was conquered by the Franks, who made it the centre of their Hispanic March. The struggle for Barcelona, however, was not yet over: the city was retaken by the Arabs in 799, then the Carolingians besieged it again from 800–801. After reconquering Barcelona, the Franks continued to press forward to expand their Spanish territories. They took Tarragona and Tortosa, gaining access to the mouth of the Ebro River in the last years of Charles' reign. Between 780 and 805, the Basques continued their resistance against the Carolingians, collaborating with any local rebellion taking place in Aquitaine and trying to retain control over the mountain passes of the Pyrenees. From 790, however, Charles asserted his authority over the Pyrenees by transforming certain Basque lords into his vassals. The stability brought by the Franks did not last for long, since soon after the death of Charles the Basques rebelled against the Carolingian authorities, together with the Gascons. During the late eighth century, as well as fighting against the Arabs in the Iberian

Peninsula, the Franks also clashed with them in the waters of the Mediterranean. After the fall of the Lombard Kingdom, the Franks conquered the islands of Corsica and Sardinia, which were followed by the Balearic Islands in 799. The Frankish warlords who had received lands in north-western Italy slowly built up significant fleets, with which they controlled the newly conquered islands and fought against the piratical activities of the Muslims until the end of Charles' reign.

The fiercest enemies of Charles were without doubt the Saxons, who resisted Frankish penetration into their lands for decades. It took thirty years of war and no less than eighteen battles for the great monarch to subdue the Germanic warriors living on the eastern borders of his territories. The Saxon Wars of Charles were a long and complex politico-military process, the Carolingians wishing to annexe most of Germany to the Frankish territories by converting to Christianity a warlike population that had remained fiercely pagan. The first campaign against the Saxons took place in 773 and did not lead to any significant results. In 775, however, Charles marched through modern Westphalia to conquer a substantial portion of the Saxons' lands. The Saxons had no unified leadership, being organized into four autonomous communities, each of which pursued their own interests, a situation that greatly favoured the Franks. By the end of 775, Charles had occupied the most important strongholds of the Saxons, but they were still determined to fight for their freedom. The following year, a major revolt broke out in those parts of Saxony that were garrisoned by Frankish troops. The rebellion was led by a capable military leader named Widukind, who for the first time was able to unite the Saxons under a single leadership. Charles, who was fighting in Italy at the time against the Lombards of Spoleto and Benevento, had to return with the bulk of his army to Germany in order to defeat the Saxons. He secured another victory, but Widukind was able to escape to Denmark, where he could count on the support of the local king. In 777, after building a permanent military camp at Karlstadt, Charles called a national assembly with the objective of integrating Saxony into the Frankish Kingdom. His political agenda worked only partially, since only a portion of the Saxon leaders and warriors agreed to be baptized as Christians and recognize Carolingian suzerainty over their lands. A major new revolt broke out in Saxony during 778, forcing Charles to invade the Saxon lands again in 779. Hoping to gain control over the newly reconquered territories, Charles divided them into missionary districts and sponsored a Roman Church programme of mass baptisms. In 782, to keep Saxony under his rule, the Frankish monarch instituted a new code of laws that contained draconian measures regarding religious issues. According to the *Capitulatio de partibus Saxoniae* (Capitulary for the Saxon Regions), for example, each Saxon pagan who refused to

Carolingian heavy cavalryman wearing corselet of mail armour (*brunia*). (*Photo and copyright by Hiwisca – Eine Familia in der Karolingerzeit*)

Carolingian heavy infantryman wearing chainmail. (*Photo and copyright by Hiwisca – Eine Familia in der Karolingerzeit*)

convert to Christianity had to be killed by the Carolingian authorities. The use of such harsh methods did nothing but cause further Saxon rebellions.

In the autumn of 782, Widukind returned to Saxony to lead a new revolt of his people. The Saxons were extremely difficult to submit militarily because they fought according to the basic principles of guerrilla warfare on a territory that was particularly inhospitable for any foreign invader. At that time, Saxony did not have any major urban centre and was mostly covered by impenetrable woods. Furthermore, the Franks had only a superficial knowledge of these wild areas, while the Saxons were perfectly used to move and fight in the woods. The Saxon communities had a harsh lifestyle and lived in connection with nature, being organized into small rural settlements whose male members were all experienced warriors and huntsmen. The Saxon fighters were skilled at skirmishing with numerically superior enemy forces and knew how to prepare deadly ambushes. Using such accomplishments, they defeated the Carolingians on several occasions, obliging them to sustain significant losses during the many campaigns that were fought in Saxony. Unable to crush the resistance of his enemies, Charles had no choice but to commit a series of atrocities and massacres. At Verden, after the outbreak of the rebellion of 782, he ordered the mass execution by beheading of 4,500 Saxon prisoners. The Carolingian monarch hoped that the 'Massacre of Verden' would break the morale of Widukind's followers, but the effect provoked by his actions was exactly the opposite. This national uprising by the Saxons lasted for three years and saw many bloody clashes, the Saxons being joined by the Frisians in their struggle. Indeed, for several months it seemed that the Franks could be defeated. In the end, however, Charles was able to prevail after employing all the military resources at his disposal. Widukind, seeing that his people risked complete extinction, finally agreed to surrender in return for a guarantee that no bodily harm would be done to him. In 785, he and his warlords agreed to be baptized, with Charles as their godfather. This symbolic act was intended by the Carolingian monarch to pacify Saxony once and for all. A peace agreement was reached with Widukind, according to which the Saxon nobles retained their social status after becoming part of the Carolingian aristocracy. Various further minor Saxon rebellions took place between 792 and 794, and again in 796, but these were crushed quite easily by the Franks because they did not include the participation of the Saxon noble warlords. By 804, after much bloodshed, Charles had finally pacified Saxony under his rule.

While campaigning against the Saxons, Charles also fought lesser-known wars in other areas of his vast realm. In 789, for example, he turned his attentions to Bavaria, deciding to remove the region's ruling duke, Tassilo III. During the previous decades, Bavaria had expanded eastwards, transforming several Slavic communities living on its borders into tributaries. Charles was interested in expanding his dominions in Central Europe and thus decided to annex Bavaria to his realm. After deposing Tassilo and forcing him to enter a monastery, he obliged the Agilolfings to renounce any claim to Bavaria and to cede all their rights over the area to the Carolingians. As had already been done with Saxony, Bavaria was subdivided into Frankish counties and a new Carolingian aristocracy was established on its territory. Bavaria, which included the territory of present-day Austria, was soon transformed into the main base of the Frankish military forces in Central Europe. From Bavaria, the Franks expanded northwards in Bohemia/Moravia and southwards in Slovenia/Croatia. In 790, the Avars invaded Bavaria from Pannonia, causing serious damage to a vast border area of the Frankish Kingdom. Charles responded by organizing a massive counter-offensive and marching along the course of the Danube, ravaging the northern half of Pannonia. Meanwhile, another Carolingian army, advancing from Italy, devastated the southern territories of the Avars. In 792, the hostilities had to be suspended before the Franks could achieve a decisive victory over the Avars due to the outbreak of another revolt by the Saxons. During the following years, a state of war continued to exist between the Franks and the Avars. The Avars were defeated on several occasions and their capital was looted twice by Carolingian troops. Most of the Avar leaders eventually accepted becoming vassals of Charles and to be baptized as Christians. In 803, what remained of the independent Avar state in Pannonia was defeated and annexed by the Franks.

With the conquest of Bavaria and Pannonia, the Carolingians established a significant presence in Central Europe and became a regional power of the vast Trans-danubian area. As such, they started to look with great interest at the lands inhabited by the Slavs, which were rich in important natural resources such as gold and silver. In 789, Charles had sent an army from Saxony into the homeland of the Slavs who lived in eastern Germany, such as the Obotrites and the Veleti. These tribes submitted without a fight and became loyal allies of the Franks. Their leaders permitted the establishment of Christian missions on their territories and did not oppose the subsequent conversion of their subjects. During the following years, the northern Slavs even collaborated with the Franks in their campaigns against the Saxons, offering the Carolingians significant help. The northern Slavs remained loyal vassals of Charles until his death, policing the frontier of Frankish territories in remote areas like the German region of Holstein. This area, which had been inhabited by the Saxons for a long time, was located just south of the Viking territories in Denmark. In 804, following the definitive defeat of the Saxons, Charles decided to assign the key region of Holstein to the Obotrite Slavs as a reward for their loyalty. The Frankish troops reached the Eider River, which marked the southern boundary of Denmark at the time, in order to secure the position of the Obotrites. Upon this, the Danish

Carolingian heavy cavalryman equipped with nasal helmet having an aventail of mail on the back. (*Photo and copyright by Novum Milites Francorum*)

monarch, Gudfred, started being concerned by the presence of the Carolingians and prepared his realm for war. During the previous years, Gudfred had already welcomed Saxon refugees, which was perceived as a personal affront by Charles. Following the failure of peace talks, Gudfred organized a successful seaborne invasion of Holstein.

Carolingian heavy infantryman bearing standard and horn; the latter was used to transmit orders from long distance. (*Photo and copyright by Hiwisca – Eine Familia in der Karolingerzeit*)

The Obotrites were rapidly defeated by the Danish Vikings, who built a wall on the southern border of Holstein – known as the Danevirke – before Charles could initiate a counter-offensive. Charles had intended to launch his attack in 810, but before this could happen, Gudfred struck first. He assembled an impressive fleet of some 200 warships and attacked Frisia, a move that was completely unexpected by the Franks. The Danes obtained a series of victories and occupied a large portion of Frisia, with the objective of annexing it to their realm. At this point, the Carolingians mobilized all their forces and moved north to repulse the invaders. Before battle could be joined, however, the Viking fleet evacuated Frisia after learning that Gudfred had been assassinated. The murder of the Danish king was the result of a palace coup, probably aimed at avoiding a direct confrontation with the Carolingians that could have been potentially destructive for Denmark. In 811, the nephew and successor of Gudfred, Hemming, signed a peace treaty with Charles. Under the terms of the settlement, the Eider River was recognized as the definitive border dividing Frankish lands from those of the Danes.

From 801, to secure the northern coastline of his realm in view of possible Viking raids, Charles tried to annex Brittany to his dominions by conducting several military campaigns in the region. These, however, obtained only partial success due to the strong resistance of the Bretons (who were called Armoricans by the Franks). Brittany was temporarily submitted by the Carolingians only after Charles' death. As we have seen, the Franks had positive relations with the northern Slavs living in present-day eastern Germany; the same could be said, more or less, for the other Slavic communities living in Bohemia/Moravia and in the northern Balkans. Following the fall of the Avar state in Pannonia, Charles favoured the emergence of permanent Slavic settlements in Bohemia and Moravia. These had very positive relations with the Frankish Kingdom and gradually developed as a unified state, which later became known as Great Moravia and came to control large territories located north of the Danube. The Bohemians and Moravians soon became Christians, a move which favoured their role as allies of the Carolingians. In the northern Balkans, following the Avars' defeat in 796, the southern Slavs became loyal tributaries of the Carolingians. Charles thus came to control Dalmatia and Slavonia, challenging the Byzantine presence in the Adriatic Sea. In 799, the Croats rebelled against Charles. They were defeated after several years of fighting and had no choice but to accept Frankish dominance in 802. When Charles died in 814, his immense dominions extended from Catalonia in the south-west to Holstein in the north-east, and from Brittany in the north-west to Dalmatia in the south-east. It was thanks to his incredible conquests that Charles later became known as Charlemagne (the French for Charles the Great).

Carolingian heavy infantryman equipped with spear and shield. (*Photo and copyright by Novum Milites Francorum*)

Carolingian standard-bearer of the heavy infantry. Note the practice of wearing a soft cap under the helmet. (*Photo and copyright by Hiwisca – Eine Familia in der Karolingerzeit*)

Chapter 5

The Carolingian Army

Since the early days of the Merovingians' rule, after the unification of the Salians with the Ripuarians, the Frankish armies comprised two different categories of warriors: the professional fighters, known as *antrustiones*, and the common soldiers, who were mobilized with the traditional Germanic levy and known as the *heerbann*. The *antrustiones* originated as the bodyguards of the various Frankish warlords, consisting of personal retinues bound to the monarch's service by oaths of loyalty. Several of them were friends or relatives of the king, and thus they pursued the same interests as the monarch. The *antrustiones* included some high-ranking officials, such as the mayor of the palace, the counts and the marshal. The counts were the most prominent nobles of the Frankish realms, controlling large portions of territory and commanding the various military contingents that were mobilized according to the *heerbann*. The marshal, meanwhile, was a single officer tasked with performing a series of important logistical duties: he was responsible for supplying and organizing the army, as well as for keeping discipline in its ranks and for supervising the construction of camps. A good number of the *antrustiones* were always deployed near the royal court, forming a private army that was placed under the direct control of the king. Several of them, however, were posted in strategic garrisons located across their realms. These were organized into units with 100 warriors each, known as *centenae*, each of which garrisoned a specific location. In the event of war, all the *antrustiones* were assembled together, forming an elite guard contingent that could number anything from a minimum of 5,000 to a maximum of 10,000 men. All the major Frankish aristocrats had their own bodyguards of *antrustiones*, which became increasingly large over time, to the point that they could rival the guard of the monarch. The general levy known as the *heerbann* was introduced in the Frankish lands during the second half of the sixth century and initially involved only the inhabitants of the cities. Soon, however, all the Frankish able-bodied freemen up to the age of 60 were obliged to serve when called to do so. The *comes*, or counts, were responsible for the general mobilization in time of war, while in time of peace, the able-bodied freemen were required to perform some auxiliary military duties such as garrisoning fortified places and repairing fortifications and other infrastructure. The poorest individuals who could not afford to equip themselves were exempted from military service, but this changed under the Carolingians when the central government started to supply weapons to the poorest subjects. After the Merovingians completed their conquest of Gaul, the *heerbann* was reduced and started to involve just one man from each family. Failure to serve was punishable by death according to law, but in most cases it resulted in a heavy fine that was calculated according to the defaulter's economic capabilities. The period of service in the general levy was not specified, but in most cases it was limited to six months because seeding and harvesting had to be performed by most Frankish freemen who had a family.

The season of military campaigning began with the annual assembly in arms, known as the *marchfield*, which took place every year on the first day of March. The soldiers mobilized with the *heerbann*, like in all the other armies of Germanic Europe, were assembled into units of ten men each that were in turn assembled together to form 'hundreds' and 'thousands', according to a decimal system. During the early Merovingian period, most of the *antrustiones* fought as heavy cavalry, with helmets and cuirasses, while the soldiers of the general levy served as medium infantry, carrying a spear and shield. However, cavalry eventually became an increasingly important component of the Frankish armies. It was for this reason that the *marchfield* started to take place every year on the first day of May – which became known as *mayfield* – in order to have adequate forage to feed the horses while on campaign. The mounted troops of the Merovingians did not use stirrups, and thus were not true cavalry from a tactical point of view. Most of the Frankish professional soldiers, in fact, were mounted infantrymen who travelled on horse but fought on foot. They had a high degree of mobility and could pursue a defeated enemy on horseback, but when fighting pitched battles, they usually acted as standard heavy infantry.

Under the Carolingians, especially with Charlemagne, cavalry became increasingly important in the Frankish armies. This was the result of the Franks' frequent contact with armies that were made up of fast-moving mounted contingents, like those of the Avars. From 864, all the Frankish freemen who owned or could obtain a horse were officially required to attend the *heerbann* as cavalrymen. The transformation of the Frankish army from an infantry force to a cavalry one was also helped by the adoption of the stirrup, which was copied from the Avars, who had employed it for a long time like the other nomadic peoples of the steppes. During the Carolingian period, compulsory military service was due from every freeman who owned four *mansi* of land, each *mansus* corresponding – more or less – to the average portion of land owned by a single Frankish family. As a result, four *mansi* were the standard extent of a minor landowner's property. During the Merovingian period, most of the Franks owned a small land property, while in the Carolingian period an increasing number of them were assigned a farm as a *benefice* (as a grant of land received from

Carolingian heavy infantryman transporting his round shield on the back. (*Photo and copyright by Novum Milites Francorum*)

Carolingian heavy infantryman employing a throwing javelin.
(*Photo and copyright by Novum Milites Francorum*)

a noble). There were also landowners who were assigned a property by the royal government. These became increasingly common with the expansion of the Frankish Kingdom, as Charlemagne sponsored the settling of his most loyal soldiers on newly conquered foreign lands (especially if located in frontier regions). These royal vassals were all required to serve as cavalry and were known as *caballarii*. The freemen who had less than four *mansi* of land had to combine with other individuals in the same economic position in order to supply one warrior to the *heerbann*. The man who

Carolingian heavy infantryman. Note the distinctive shape of the umbo (the shield's boss) that could be employed as an offensive weapon. (*Photo and copyright by De vita aetate carolingorum*)

Carolingian heavy cavalryman wearing a short-sleeved corselet of mail armour. (*Photo and copyright by De vita aetate carolingorum*)

was chosen to serve had his equipment and rations provided by those who remained at home. In 807, this system was slightly modified, with each man holding at least two *mansi* of land now obliged to serve. The standard organization of the various contingents remained decimal, but the period of service in the general levy was fixed at three months. In case of emergency, military service could be required more than

Carolingian warlord armed with a sword and white leather scabbard. (*Photo and copyright by Hiwisca – Eine Familia in der Karolingerzeit*)

once a year, but with a pause of forty days between each period of campaigning. Each mobilized warrior had to carry his own rations for a period of three months and had to equip himself according to his economic capabilities, with the poorest individuals able to receive some weapons from the central government.

The various military contingents were commanded by *comites* (counts), who became prominent politico-military figures within the administration of Charlemagne. Each count was a government functionary, chosen from the aristocrats who were extremely loyal to the Carolingians, who exercised state power in the *comitatus*, or county, of the Frankish Kingdom that was assigned to him by the monarch. The old *duces* (dukes) lost most of their previous importance after the creation of the counts, since they were at the orders of the latter and controlled smaller territories. The frontier counties of the Frankish territories, which were exposed to foreign invasions and raids, were given a special status by Charlemagne and became known as *marcae*, or marches. The marches latter were garrisoned by significant military forces and had several strongholds on their territory, which had defensive functions but were also employed as military bases for offensive operations. Each march was ruled by a *markgraf* (marquise), who was responsible for defending the frontier of his domains and for organizing a first line of defence in case of enemy invasions. The growing tactical importance of cavalry in the Frankish armies made Charlemagne create a new high-ranking official known as the *comes stabuli*, or constable, who was responsible for the maintenance of the royal herds that provided mounts to a significant portion of the Frankish cavalry. The logistical organization of the Frankish forces was greatly improved by Charlemagne, who created a massive baggage train equipped with leather-covered hooded ox-carts. These could transport any kind of military material and were waterproofed so that they could be ferried across rivers.

Charlemagne completely reorganized the professional military forces of the *antrustiones*, transforming them into a proper and powerful royal guard. They were no longer tasked only with bodyguard duties, but had to act as the standing nucleus of the Frankish army. Consisting of professional soldiers serving full-time, they had to be ready to march within twelve hours of being called. The royal guardsmen were all *caballarii* and were heavily equipped, so they could move very rapidly from their garrisons at court in order to face an unexpected foreign invasion. In case of expansionist campaigns, they made up the core of the Frankish forces and provided leadership to the non-professional units recruited with the general levy. The new Frankish royal guard organized by Charlemagne was known as the *scara*. Its members initially served as mounted infantrymen, but over time they became the first Frankish soldiers to be equipped with stirrups. The *scara* was garrisoned near the king's palace, and thus its elite soldiers were also known as *palatini*. It was divided into three distinct bodies, which were differentiated by the seniority of their components: the *scholares*, the *schola* and the *milites aulae regiae*. The *scholares* were the older veterans and formed the inner guard of the king, while the *schola* consisted of younger veterans who guarded the monarch when he was not in his palace. The *milites aulae regiae*, meanwhile, were junior royal guardsmen who garrisoned the royal residences. Like all the *caballarii* of the Frankish army, those of the royal guard were proto-feudal knights, providing their military service in exchange for receiving a grant of land. The members of the *scara* underwent intensive military training and were highly disciplined. The *milites aulae regiae* performed a series of ceremonial duties and were equipped in imitation of the contemporary guard corps of the Byzantine Empire, with old-fashioned helmets and cuirasses. The members of the *schola* and the *scholares*, instead, were equipped as heavy cavalrymen with a cuirass (*brunia*) of chainmail or scale armour. Charlemagne's heavy cavalry did not charge with spears placed firmly beneath the armpit, a tactic which only became widespread in later times. Instead, spears were still thrust with a swing of the hand under or over arm, as in previous centuries.

Under Charlemagne, the Frankish army became an extremely multi-ethnic military force, the various territories that were conquered by the Carolingians all being required to provide some military contingents to their new overlords. These foreign troops brought with them different military traditions, which were all absorbed into the Frankish military organization. The Lombards, who were the first to be submitted by Charlemagne, had quite sophisticated military structures in their kingdom. Initially, the Lombard troops were organized on a tribal basis, with each clan, or *fara*, mobilizing its able-bodied free men in case of war. The Lombard territories in Italy eventually started to be organized as duchies that were sub-divided into territorial entities known as *sculdascie*. Each of the latter was controlled by an official named by the duke, who was responsible for the mobilization of the general levy. Initially, all Lombard free men considered military service a great honour and always responded to the calls made by their monarch, but over time, and with the frequent outbreak of civil wars, this situation changed. Many free men started to buy exemptions from compulsory military service by corrupting central government officials, which significantly depleted the available manpower. The Lombard monarchs responded to this by recruiting increasing numbers of non-Lombard soldiers and expanding the number of professional warriors who formed their personal retinue. These full-time fighters were known as *gasindi* and consisted of elite heavy cavalry who were bound to the king's service by oaths of loyalty. In 750, all the able-bodied free men of the Lombard Kingdom were divided into four categories according to the quantity of land they owned, with the members of each of these categories serving in the

Carolingian heavy infantryman wearing scale armour for protection of the upper legs.
(*Photo and copyright by Jurgen Ritter*)

Carolingian medium infantryman with nasal helmet. (*Photo and copyright by Novum Milites Francorum*)

Carolingian medium infantryman equipped with spear and shield. (*Photo and copyright by Hiwisca – Eine Familia in der Karolingerzeit*)

army with a different panoply. The warriors of the first category served as heavy cavalrymen, those of the second as medium cavalry, the third as light cavalry and the fourth as infantry. Those subjects who did not own any land also served in the army, being divided into three categories (medium cavalry, light cavalry and infantry) according to their economic capabilities. As is clear from the above, the Lombard army was mostly a cavalry force that was heavily influenced by the tactics of the Avars. Many of the Lombard cavalry, however, fought as mounted infantry rather than as proper horsemen.

The Visigoths of Spain and Septimania became a significant component of the Frankish armies during Charlemagne's reign. Originally they had a military organization based on tribal subdivisions, with each clan mobilizing its own armed contingent that was known as a *thiufa*. Each *thiufa* had a decimal structure and thus comprised several 'hundreds' of warriors. The contingents mobilized with the general levy were commanded by dukes, some of whom could be more powerful than the king. The king, however, could count on his personal retinue that was made up of professional warriors known as *fideles*. These were extremely loyal to the monarch and could sometimes be freed slaves. The various Visigothic nobles – most notably the dukes – had their own bodyguards, who consisted of *bucellarii* and *saiones*. The *bucellarii* were professional soldiers paid with money, while the *saiones*, although also professional warriors, were paid with goods such as pieces of equipment. Over time, the Visigoths developed a new social class of full-time warriors who served in exchange for receiving a grant of land. These were known as *gardingi* and were lesser nobles who had to equip themselves as heavy cavalrymen in time of war. Curiously, the Visigothic free men were not only obliged to serve in person after general mobilization but also had to provide some of their slaves – if they owned any – for service in the army. The slaves made up a good proportion of the infantry, while most of the cavalry consisted of heavily equipped mounted infantrymen. By the time of the Arab conquest of the Iberian Peninsula, the Visigothic forces comprised another two categories of troops in addition to those described above: the *spathari* and the *leudes*. The *spathari* were aristocrats of lower rank who made up a noble bodyguard that was placed at the direct orders of the king, whereas the *leudes* were military colonists who had been assigned a grant of land on the frontiers of the Visigothic Kingdom. The *leudes* performed as border troops in exchange for receiving a land property from the central government. Living on the frontiers with their own families, they were highly motivated to repulse foreign raids and invasions. The *leudes* were quite numerous in northern Spain, where the Visigothic Kingdom bordered with the Frankish lands and the territory of the warlike Basques.

Carolingian medium infantryman wearing a helmet with aventail of chainmail on the back. (*Photo and copyright by Hiwisca – Eine Familia in der Karolingerzeit*)

Carolingian swordsman equipped with round shield.
(*Photo and copyright by Hiwisca – Eine Familia in der Karolingerzeit*)

The Frankish army comprised several other foreign contingents, some of which came from the territory of Gaul. The major urban centres of present-day southern France, located south of the Loire River, continued to be inhabited by flourishing Gallo-Roman communities until the end of Charlemagne's reign. The Frankish presence in southern Gaul, in fact, was never as significant as it was in the territories north of the Loire. This meant that the Gallo-Romans contributed some sizeable contingents to the formation of the Frankish armies, since they were subject to taxation and military service. The Gallo-Roman troops were raised according to the old Late Roman system structured on dioceses, which continued to exist well after the fall of the Western Empire. According to contemporary sources, only the Gallo-Romans who owned some land were subject to compulsory military service. They were commanded by members of their urban aristocracy, who had their own personal retinues of professional warriors (*pueri*) exactly like the Frankish warlords. Before being conquered by the Merovingians, the lands of south-eastern Gaul had been occupied by the Burgundians, and were progressively absorbed into the Frankish military forces. This process was quite natural, since the Burgundians had more or less the same military organization and equipment as the Franks. Eventually, they even started to provide some elite soldiers for service in the Carolingian royal *scara* guard. The same happened with the Alamanni, who had become fully integrated into the Frankish army by the end of the eighth century. As we have seen, the Franks never established any real hegemony over the Bretons who lived in the isolated peninsula of Brittany, although these sometimes provided auxiliary contingents to the Carolingians. Breton warfare was a mix of Celtic and Late Roman traditions, including some Alan elements. During the Late Empire, the Roman authorities had settled some sizeable Alan communities on the territory of Brittany in order to employ them as military colonists. The Alans were a nomadic people of the steppes, having a lot in common with the Sarmatians; as a result, they brought to Brittany their military traditions based on the use of mounted archers and heavily armoured cavalrymen. By the time of Charlemagne's reign, the Breton contingents in Frankish service mostly consisted of mounted skirmishers armed with javelins, who were supplemented by a limited number of elite heavy cavalry equipped with full armour, like the cataphracts of the Late Roman Army (their horses also being armoured). Curiously, the Breton heavy cavalry was not armed with spears but with throwing javelins.

The warlike Gascons and Basques, just like the Bretons, were never completely submitted by the Franks. Nevertheless, they did make up a significant portion of the armed forces that could be levied by the Carolingians in the wild region of Aquitaine. The Gascons fought as excellent mounted skirmishers and were usually equipped with throwing javelins, whereas the Basques could deploy the best mountain infantry

Carolingian medium infantryman armed with spear, sword and knife. (*Photo and copyright by Novum Milites Francorum*)

Carolingian medium infantryman armed with throwing javelin and *seax*. (*Photo and copyright by Novum Milites Francorum*)

Carolingian medium infantryman equipped with spear and shield. (*Photo and copyright by Jurgen Ritter*)

of Carolingian Europe. Most of the Basque warriors were javelinmen, but there were also significant numbers of archers and slingers. The Saxons and the Thuringians had already provided auxiliaries to the Franks during the Merovingian period, but they only became a permanent component of the Frankish army after Charlemagne completed the bloody conquest of their territories. The Saxons and Thuringians had less heavy troops than the Franks, but were superior to them with regard to missile troops. The Saxon archers, in particular, were famous for their combat abilities as light skirmishers. The Bavarians always had the same military organization and equipment as the Franks, so their absorption into the Carolingian armies was quite an easy process. It should be noted, however, that the Bavarians had given more importance to cavalry in their troops well before the Franks, having come into contact at an early date with the Avars (which enabled them to copy the stirrup from the nomadic steppes people). During the late reign of Charlemagne, the Frankish forces started to contain a certain number of Slavic and Avar auxiliaries. The Slavic troops mostly consisted of lightly armed infantry spearmen, who proved their worth in the wars fought against the Saxons. Over time, the Slavs began to adopt some pieces of equipment used by the Franks – such as swords – which significantly improved their ability in combat. The Avars provided some mounted contingents to the Carolingians only after having been partly defeated by them, including some excellent heavy cavalrymen equipped with lamellar armour and trained to charge with the lance thanks to the use of stirrups. The Avars, of course, also deployed contingents of mounted archers armed with powerful composite bows. The military forces of the papacy always remained the most loyal ally of the Carolingians. According to contemporary sources, the pope was defended by a trusted guard made up of Germanic warriors; originally these were mercenaries, but it is probable that by the time of Charlemagne's reign they could include a significant number of Frankish professional soldiers.

Chapter 6

The Decline of the Carolingians, 814–987

The reign of Charlemagne was characterized by the many wars described in the previous chapter, but also saw a series of important political events that permanently changed the history of continental Europe. In 799, Pope Leo III was in danger of being killed during a popular revolt that took place in the city of Rome. He was left with no other choice than to leave Italy to save his life, travelling to the court of Charlemagne. The great Frankish king agreed to restore Leo III's power in Rome and went to Italy at the head of an army in November 800. Once in the former capital of the Roman Empire, however, Charlemagne obliged the weakened Leo III to crown him Emperor of the Romans in Saint Peter's Basilica on Christmas Day of 800. This event had enormous significance, since it transformed the Frankish Kingdom into the direct heir of the Roman Empire. Charlemagne had occupied most of continental Europe during the previous three decades and had been seeking some politico-religious legitimacy for his conquests. His victories had to be perceived as the direct result of God's will to restore the political institution of the Roman Empire in Christian Europe. From the day of Charlemagne's coronation, the Frankish Kingdom became a new political entity, having a superior moral stature compared with the other states existing on its borders. It assumed the new denomination of the Holy Roman Empire, which continued to be used by the successors of Charlemagne for almost a millennium. The new Frankish Empire was 'Holy' because it was tasked with protecting Christianity from the menace represented by other religions and because it had been blessed by God with the intermediation of the Pope. Furthermore, it was 'Roman' because it wanted to be recognized as the direct heir of Imperial Rome and its Empire's universalistic ambitions.

Charlemagne was a great monarch who totally reformed the institutions of his state and thereby dragged Europe into the decisive centuries of the Middle Ages. The Frankish ruler had a multi-ethnic itinerant court that was constantly on the move, but also established some magnificent palaces at Aachen, Ingelheim, Frankfurt and Mainz that soon became important administrative and learning centres. The top-ranking figures of the Carolingian court were the chaplain (who was responsible for all ecclesiastical affairs in the Frankish Empire) and the count palatine (who commanded the military units of the Royal Guard that were part of Charlemagne's household).

There was also a chancellor, tasked with producing all the written documents that were promulgated by the Carolingian government. As already explained above, the counts made up the backbone of the Frankish politico-military administration: they controlled the various regions of the Carolingian Empire, which were subdivided into territorial units known as *centenae*. Each *centenae* had its own local official known as a vicar, who was responsible for the administration of justice, the levying of soldiers, the repair of roads and bridges, the collecting of taxes and the enforcement of the 'capitularies', or orders, promulgated by the Carolingian chancellery. Originally, the vicars were royal agents appointed by the court, but over time they started to be local minor aristocrats and their offices became hereditary. This favoured the spreading of corruption, a problem to which Charlemagne responded in 802 by creating the *Missi Dominici*. These were high officials who operated in couples (one was an ecclesiastic official and the other a secular official) and were tasked with inspecting the local administrations of the Frankish state. The *Missi Dominici* were constantly on the move, since they had to make four inspection journeys every year in order to keep under royal control all the territories of the Carolingian Empire. Being appointed directly by the king, they were specifically required to counter the spreading of corruption and to signal any element that could reveal the imminent outbreak of local rebellions. Sometimes, the *Missi Dominici* were supported in their activities by the *caballarii*, who were also known as the *Vassi Dominici* because they were royal vassals. Around 780, Charlemagne completely reformed the judicial system of his state by creating a new category of legal experts known as *scabini*, seven of whom supported each count in the administration of justice. In 802, Charlemagne ordered the writing down and updating of all Frankish laws, thereby producing a new code that was distributed in every county.

Charlemagne also reformed the coinage system of the Frankish lands, substituting gold with silver and controlling the composition and value of the new coins. He tried to improve the agricultural capabilities of his domains by enacting a specific text known as the *Capitulare de villis*, which contained a series of rules and regulations on how to manage land properties, domestic animals and rural justice in the most effective way. The early years of the ninth century saw great cultural changes in Europe, which are collectively known as the Carolingian Renaissance. This was sponsored by Charlemagne, who was constantly striving to propitiate a new flowering of scholarship and arts in his domains. Monastic schools and *scriptoria* (centres for book-copying) were established in every corner of the Frankish Empire, while the Carolingians also encouraged clerics to translate Christian religious texts from Latin into the local vernacular languages of Germanic Europe. Many thousands of literary works produced during antiquity were copied and thus saved from oblivion during the

Carolingian spearman. Note the simple manufacture of the helmet. (*Photo and copyright by De vita aetate carolingorum*)

Carolingian Renaissance. Charlemagne invited several important intellectuals to become part of his court in order to carry out his ambitious cultural programme. These included the Anglo-Saxon Alcuin of York, the Lombard Paul the Deacon, the Frankish Einhard (who was his personal biographer) and many other scholars of great value. Charlemagne spent most of his later years studying under the guidance of such intellectuals, learning how to read, a skill that was quite exceptional for a Germanic monarch of the time. The monarch also promoted the creation of a new form of writing, the Carolingian minuscule, which was easy both to learn and to write. His ambition was to spread a unified form of writing across all his vast domains in order to avoid the further development of local writings, which could be complicated to understand for readers who had little familiarity with them. As regards the church, Charlemagne worked hard to improve the clergy's skills and moral quality, as well as to standardize liturgical practices. He also exerted complete control over the religious authorities and properties of the Holy Roman Empire, fighting against every form of heresy and against what remained of paganism. Several of the capitularies promulgated by the Carolingian chancellery dealt with religious issues, going into a high level of detail.

In 806, Charlemagne made the first provisions for the division of the

Merovingian light infantryman armed with spear and throwing javelin. (*Photo by Julien Souris, copyright by Lupi Austrasiae*)

Merovingian light infantryman wearing a soft cap. (*Photo by Julien Souris, copyright by Lupi Austrasiae*)

Merovingian light infantryman wearing a fur cap. (*Photo by Julien Souris, copyright by Lupi Austrasiae*)

Carolingian light spearman. (*Photo by Julien Souris, copyright by Gisna Missi Dominici*)

Carolingian Empire upon his death. Frankish territories were to be divided between his three legitimate sons – Charles the Younger, Pepin and Louis – according to the traditional method prescribed by the Salic Law. During 810 and 811, however, both Pepin and Charles the Younger died, meaning that Louis, known as 'the Pious' because of his temperament, remained as the sole heir to the Carolingian throne. In 813, Louis was crowned co-emperor by his father and started to administer the Frankish territories on the behalf of Charlemagne. In January 814, Charlemagne fell ill with pleurisy and died a few days later, having been supreme ruler of the Franks for forty-seven years. He was buried in the magnificent Aachen Cathedral that he had built some years before. As prescribed in his testament, he left most of his personal wealth to the church, with the precise request that it be used for charity. Louis the Pious thus became monarch of one of the largest empires that history had ever seen, but he soon started to experience a series of difficulties. Being under strong pressure from his own three sons, since he was no longer young, in 817 the new emperor was forced to issue a special decree – known as the *Ordinatio Imperii* – that laid out plans for an orderly dynastic succession. Lothair, his first son, was crowned co-emperor and was promised that he would rule over most of the Frankish dominions. Pepin, the second son, was proclaimed King of Aquitaine, while Louis, the youngest son, was made King of Bavaria. Both Pepin and Louis were subordinate to Lothair, and if they died childless their domains would have been assigned to their older brother. The division contained in the *Ordinatio Imperii* thus prescribed the existence of a single emperor who was to rule over two subordinate kings. While this was done to preserve the unity of the Frankish Empire, it made both Pepin and Louis extremely unhappy since they disliked Lothair. It thus soon became apparent that the proposed division of the Frankish territories could not work. The situation was not helped by the fact that the succession plans did not assign any land to the ambitious Bernard, who was a grandson of Charlemagne; he was the illegitimate son of Louis the Pious' deceased brother, Pepin, and had been appointed ruler of Italy after his father's death in 810. Furthermore, there was the problem represented by the existence of another son of Louis the Pious – Charles the Bald – who was born from the emperor's second marriage.

Soon after the implementing of the *Ordinatio Imperii*, Bernard started plotting against Louis the Pious in order to break away from the Frankish Empire as King of Italy. The emperor reacted rapidly and moved towards the Alps at the head of a large army. Intimidated by Louis the Pious' swift mobilization, Bernard chose to surrender rather than fight and was captured. He died a few days after having been blinded as a traitor. From 816, Louis the Pious had to face a series of local rebellions across his empire. The first to rise up in revolt were the Slavs, initially in north-eastern Germany and then also in the northern Balkans. The Slavic communities fighting against the Carolingians were supported by the Danish Vikings in the north and by the Bulgars in the south. The Bulgars had taken the place of the Avars following the latter's defeat and had established their own nomadic state in the heart of the Balkans. In southern Italy, Louis the Pious also had to face the Lombards from the Duchy of Benevento, while in the Iberian Peninsula he had to deploy significant military contingents to retain control of the Pyrenees due to the outbreak of a major Basque and Gascon rebellion. The latter uprising was suppressed only after the emperor led an army into the rebels' territory. Louis the Pious also had to campaign against the Bretons, who were no longer happy to accept the formal overlordship of the Franks. In 829, the emperor decided to modify the territorial division prescribed by the *Ordinatio Imperii* by assigning Alamannia to the young Charles the Bald. This provoked the outbreak of a major civil war, with both Pepin of Aquitaine and Louis of Bavaria revolting against their father and capturing the emperor. Louis the Pious was left with no choice other than to promise his two rebellious sons that they would receive greater shares of his inheritance. At this point, Lothair decided to march against his two younger brothers as he strongly opposed any modification of the *Ordinatio Imperii*. However, the Frankish population rose up in revolt against Lothair before he could mobilize his troops, forcing him to end the hostilities. Disgraced and humiliated, he was banished to Italy.

Just two years after these events, in 832, a fresh civil war broke out within the Frankish Empire. Both Pepin of Aquitaine and Louis of Bavaria rebelled against their father, invading several key areas of the Frankish heartlands. The emperor responded by making a new division of his territories, according to which Lothair would inherit most of the Frankish Empire except for Aquitaine, which would be assigned to Charles the Bald. In 833, however, Lothair decided to join his two brothers in their struggle against Louis the Pious. The emperor tried to mobilize an army, but when the moment came to face Lothair, his troops changed sides. The following year, despite having been humiliated by his sons, Louis the Pious was able to regain control of his empire and forced Lothair to return to Italy. Two years later, a new division of the Carolingian lands took place, according to which Lothair was deprived of all his territory except for Italy, with the rest of his lands going to Charles the Bald. In 837, Louis the Pious assigned a significant portion of Germany to Charles the Bald, which caused another uprising by Louis of Bavaria. Then in 838, following the death of his second son, Pepin, the emperor also assigned Aquitaine to his favourite son, Charles the Bald. However, the nobles of Aquitaine did not respect the decision of Louis the Pious, electing Pepin's son, Pepin II, as the new King of Aquitaine. Yet another full-scale civil war then broke out, with both Louis of Bavaria

Carolingian light infantryman wearing Phrygian cap. (*Photo and copyright by Jurgen Ritter*)

Carolingian light spearman. Note the shape of the shield, which was a peculiarity adopted during the Carolingian period. (*Photo and copyright by Novum Milites Francorum*)

Carolingian light spearman. Most of the Carolingian infantry comprised soldiers equipped like the one shown here. (*Photo and copyright by Hiwisca – Eine Familia in der Karolingerzeit*)

(who started to be known as Louis the German) and Pepin II marching against the emperor. Lothair allied with his father in exchange for the emperor's promise to make a new division of the imperial lands. This division, the last one made by Louis the Pious, assigned the eastern half of the empire (including Italy) to Lothair and the western half to Charles the Bald. In 840, Louis the Pious defeated both Pepin II of Aquitaine and Louis the German, restoring peace in his domains, but he fell ill soon after and died on 20 June 840. The death of Louis marked the end of the Carolingian Empire's unity, as a new civil war then broke out across the Frankish territories, with Lothair allying himself with Pepin II against Louis the German and Charles the Bald. In 841, at the Battle of Fontenoy, Louis and Charles won a decisive victory over Lothair and Pepin II. One year later, in 842, Louis the German and Charles the Bald secured their alliance by declaring Lothair unfit to rule with the Oaths of Strasbourg. This was an extremely important political act, but also had a great cultural importance because Louis the German swore his oath in Romance (an early form of French) so that the soldiers of Charles the Bald could understand him, while Charles the Bald swore his oath in Germanic so that the soldiers of Louis the German could understand him. For the first time, some early forms of the future French and German languages had been used on an official occasion.

In 843, the civil war came to an end with the signing of the Treaty of Verdun, which divided the Frankish Empire between the sons of Louis the Pious. Lothair retained the imperial title, but was assigned a narrow strip of land located in the centre of the Frankish territories that extended from Frisia in the north to Provence in the south. He was also assigned the Frankish lands in Italy. Louis the German was assigned all the Carolingian territories located east of the Rhine (Saxony, Alamannia and Bavaria), while Charles the Bald was assigned most of Gaul. Pepin II continued to rule Aquitaine, but only as a loyal vassal of Charles the Bald. Louis the German had thus received the territories that later evolved to become Germany, while Charles the Bald was assigned the lands that eventually became France. The new realm of Lothair, due to its geographical features, was almost impossible to defend and thus was militarily weak. In 855, following Lothair's death, the territories that had made up his realm were divided between his three sons: Louis inherited Italy and the imperial title, Lothair II inherited present-day Lorraine (an area that started to be known as Lotharingia) and Charles inherited Burgundy. In 858, the dissatisfied Louis allied himself with his uncle Louis the German against his brother, Lothair II, and the latter's ally, Charles the Bald. Another civil conflict fought between Carolingians thus began, which ended in 862 with no clear winners. One year later, Charles of Burgundy died without direct heirs and his realm was inherited by his brother, Louis. In 869, Lothair II also died without a direct successor and his kingdom was divided

Carolingian light infantryman equipped with spear and round shield.
(*Photo and copyright by Jurgen Ritter*)

Carolingian spearman wearing a simple skull cap made of wool. (*Photo and copyright by De vita aetate carolingorum*)

between Charles the Bald and Louis the German through the Treaty of Meerssen. Louis, the only surviving son of Lothair, died in 875 after having named Carloman – the eldest son of Louis the German – as his heir. His last will, however, was not fully respected, with Charles the Bald being crowned emperor by the pope instead of Carloman and annexing Italy to his dominions. After several decades of internecine conflict, only two Frankish kingdoms remained: the western one of Charles the Bald and the eastern one of Louis the German.

In 876, Louis the German died and Charles the Bald tried to occupy the eastern half of the Carolingian territories. His invasion, however, failed due to the strong opposition of Louis the German's sons. After repelling Charles the Bald's attack, the three sons of Louis the German – Louis the Younger, Carloman of Bavaria and Charles the Fat – divided their father's domains among themselves. In 877, Charles the Bald died and was succeeded by his son, Louis the Stammerer, who had serious health problems and died after just two years of rule. The former domains of Charles the Bald were then divided between Louis the Stammerer's two sons: Louis III – who lost the title of emperor – received the territories of northern Gaul, while Carloman was assigned the lands of southern Gaul (becoming known as Carloman of Aquitaine). As regards Italy, after Charles the Bald's death it was given to Carloman of Bavaria. When Carloman of Bavaria died in 880 without direct heirs, his domains were inherited by his younger brother, Charles the Fat. In 881 and 882, Louis the Younger and Louis III also died without direct heirs. This greatly advantaged Charles the Fat, who annexed the domains of Louis the Younger, while those of Louis III were occupied by Carloman of Aquitaine. In 884, Carloman of Aquitaine suffered a mortal wound while hunting and died, whereupon his large territorial possessions in Gaul were annexed by Charles the Fat, who already had the imperial title since 881. Thanks to a series of unexpected circumstances, Charles the Fat thus came to control all the Frankish territories in 884 and thus briefly reunified the Carolingian Empire under his rule. The closing years of the ninth century saw the Frankish territories coming under increasing Viking pressure and a progressive weakening of the central government. The various nobles of the Carolingian realm started to act as independent rulers in their domains: they built fortifications without asking permission from the imperial authorities, collected taxes in an autonomous manner and did not contribute to the formation of the imperial army. The socio-political process known as feudalism was developing rapidly across Western Europe, leading to a decisive fragmentation of the territorial entities that had emerged during the previous centuries. The single warlords, ruling from their castles located around the realm, became much more powerful than the central government; the latter lost most of its original prerogatives, also to the advantage of the church.

Carolingian spearman transporting his shield on his back. (*Photo and copyright by Jurgen Ritter*)

Carolingian spearman equipped with a round shield. (*Photo and copyright by Hiwisca – Eine Familia in der Karolingerzeit*)

Carolingian swordsman. (*Photo and copyright by Jurgen Ritter*)

Charles the Fat died in 888, leaving behind a Carolingian Empire that was soon shattered by yet another civil war, which was fought between his warlike heirs. By the end of the hostilities, the once solid Frankish Empire had been divided into six smaller realms. Three of these – roughly corresponding to modern France, Germany and Italy – progressively emerged as significant powers. The Kingdom of France was ruled by Count Odo of Paris, who came from a secondary branch of the Carolingians and initiated his own new dynasty, whose members were known as Robertians because they were descended from Odo's father, Robert the Strong. Germany came under the control of Arnulf of Carinthia, who was a nephew of Charles the Fat. The Kingdom of Italy, meanwhile, entered a long phase of political chaos: for almost a century, it was ruled by local nobles of Frankish descent such as Berengar of Friuli and Guy of Spoleto. The semi-Carolingian dynasty of the Robertians governed the Kingdom of France until 987, when the last of its exponents died without heirs and was succeeded by Hugh Capet. Hugh was the eldest son of Count Hugh of Paris and initiated the new dynasty of the Capetians, the term being derived from Hugh Capet's nickname, which meant 'wearing a cape'. The Carolingians of Germany were extinguished by 911 upon the death of the son of Arnulf of Carinthia. They were succeeded by the short-lived House of Franconia, which was in turn replaced by the warlike Ottonian dynasty in 919. The Kingdom of Italy remained independent until 951, when it was invaded by the Ottonians. As for the title of Holy Roman Emperor, it ceased to have any importance after the death of Charles the Fat until it was assigned to the Ottonians in 962.

Chapter 7

The Viking Menace, 799–987

France, together with England, was one of the main targets of the Scandinavian raids during the two centuries of what became known as the Viking Age. Normandy, in particular, was greatly exposed to the attacks of the Scandinavian raiders due to its peculiar geographical position; being a peninsula stretching from northern France towards southern England, it was a perfect location for Viking naval bases. Its name derives from 'Northmannia', a term that can be translated as 'Land of the Norsemen'. Some early Viking incursions in France took place during the very last years of the reign of Charlemagne, but it was under Charles the Bald that they became a significant problem for the French monarchy. The first recorded Scandinavian attack in France took place in 799, and was soon followed by several others. In response to these early raids, around 810, Charlemagne organized a form of coastal defence in the northern regions of his empire, but this was never fully implemented. In 820, during the reign of his son, Louis the Pious, a major Scandinavian incursion was repulsed at the mouth of the Seine River. In 834, the Vikings launched a new attack against Frisia, on the territory of present-day Netherlands, which achieved great success. The following years saw an escalation of raids, with Antwerp, Rouen and Nantes all being attacked by the Vikings, who were exploiting the weakness of the Frankish military system caused by its heavy involvement in the ongoing internecine conflicts. In March 845, a large fleet of Danish Vikings, with 120 warships, entered the Seine under command of Ragnar Lodbrok. The target of the raiders was Paris, one of the richest urban centres of France. Charles the Bald, determined to fight to death in order to defend the city, rapidly mobilized his forces, dividing them into two parts: one was deployed on the eastern bank of the Seine, with the other on the western bank. At that time Paris was still relatively small, not extending beyond the Ile de la Cité, a natural river island located in the middle of the Seine. After defeating one of the two Frankish armies and killing all the captured enemies in order to spread terror, Ragnar and his men landed on the Ile de la Cité on Easter Sunday. The Scandinavians plundered Paris with great violence, killing many civilians. After several days, having obtained everything they wanted, they decided to leave the city, partly because a plague had broken out inside their camp (at that time, the banks of the Seine were covered by marshes, providing a quite inhospitable environment).

Carolingian light infantryman armed with throwing javelins: one longer javelin and three shorter ones. (*Photo and copyright by Hiwisca – Eine Familia in der Karolingerzeit*)

Carolingian light infantryman armed with short *seax*.
(*Photo and copyright by Hiwisca – Eine Familia in der Karolingerzeit*)

Before returning home, however, the Vikings obliged Charles the Bald to pay an immense sum of money: 7,000 French pounds of gold and silver. This was just the first 'danegeld' tribute paid by the Frankish monarchs to the Vikings, and it was soon followed by several others.

In the 840s, the Vikings attacked and pillaged several locations in Normandy, including Rouen, with a predilection for the richest religious sites. Thanks to the presence of many navigable rivers, the Vikings could easily move across northern and central France. The Franks were taken by surprise by their ability to sail up-river, being able to do very little to counter their attacks in any effective way. By penetrating deeply into the very heart of France, the Viking raiders soon realized that the country could easily become a land of conquest for them. Over time, the Vikings started to attack the interior areas of the Franks' territory with more frequency and with larger numbers of warships. The Frankish military system, based on elite field armies that were too large to be moved rapidly, lacked the flexibility to create highly mobile task forces that could deal with the Scandinavian raids taking place along the rivers. In 864, Charles the Bald tried to resolve this problem by issuing the Edict of Pistres, which contained a series of practical measures that were aimed at protecting French cities and rural areas from the attacks of the Vikings. With this edict, the Frankish monarch created a large force of cavalry that served on a permanent basis as a special anti-raider corps. All his subjects who were able-bodied and who owned a horse had to enlist in the new cavalry force and could be called to serve at very short notice by the royal authorities. The high mobility of cavalry was intended to counter the rapidity of the Scandinavian raids and enabled the Franks to attack the Viking warriors before they could re-embark on their warships and leave France. The Edict of Pistres also contained other important measures, such as an order to build fortified bridges at all the towns located on navigable rivers. Such bridges were intended to prevent the Vikings from sailing into the interior areas of France as well as from transporting large booties on their ships after completing their incursions. Unfortunately for the Franks, however, most of the local communities did not have the necessary resources to build new fortified bridges, so only a few of them were actually constructed. The edict enacted by Charles the Bald also prohibited all trade in weapons with the Scandinavians. Selling horses to the Vikings was also forbidden, and any infraction to the new measures was punishable by death. Charles the Bald's main objective was to prevent the Vikings from establishing permanent bases in his realm. Following the Edict of Pistres, many nobles started to build castles and fortifications on their territories in order to defend their peasant communities from the constant threat of Viking invasion. The building of private castles did nothing but reduce the power of the central government and the control that the king had over

Merovingian archer armed with wooden longbow. (*Photo by Julien Souris, copyright by Lupi Austrasiae*)

Carolingian archer equipped with leather quiver.
(Photo and copyright by Hiwisca – Eine Familia in der Karolingerzeit)

Carolingian archer with his round shield on his back. (*Photo and copyright by Novum Milites Francorum*)

the many nobles of the Kingdom of France, who became increasingly autonomous, ruling as local monarchs.

During their incursions against Normandy, the Vikings learned that the nearby region of Brittany resented Frankish rule and were thus able to conclude a military alliance with the Bretons. The Bretons were of Celtic descent and had never been fully subjugated by the Franks. As we have seen, they had strong cultural links with the Britons of Wales and had always tried to preserve their autonomy as much as possible. To counter the Viking colonization of Normandy and to block the initiatives of the alliance between the Scandinavians and Bretons, Charles the Bald created a new march (military region) on the eastern borders of Normandy. This was garrisoned by significant military forces and was put under the control of Robert the Strong, who was one of the most experienced Frankish warlords. In 866, a joint Viking and Breton force launched a massive incursion against the territory of the new march, raiding strategically important areas including Anjou and Maine. Robert the Strong responded by mobilizing his troops and by asking for the help of other powerful Frankish nobles (most notably Rainulf I, Duke of Aquitaine). The Frankish forces, mostly consisting of cavalry, succeeded in intercepting the Viking and Breton raiders before they could re-embark on their warships and go back to their bases by sailing along the Loire River. A violent pitched battle was fought, which resulted in a disaster for the Franks, whose forces were crushed and suffered severe losses, with both Robert the Strong and Rainulf of Aquitaine being killed. In 867, after such a severe defeat, Charles the Bald had no choice but to come to terms with his enemies. He recognized the leader of the Bretons as King of Brittany and ceded the Cotentin Peninsula to them. Despite this, the Vikings continued to ravage the valley of the Loire during the following years: Bourges, Orléans and Angers were all sacked. After their previous success, the Scandinavians launched another three minor incursions against Paris during the 860s. In response to these attacks, Charles the Bald promulgated the already mentioned Edict of Pistres. The edict was applied with a certain degree of efficiency in the Ile de la Cité, where two new fortified bridges were built to stop the longships of the Viking raiders, one on each side of the island, across the Seine. Paris was heavily fortified during the 870s, in anticipation of future Scandinavian attacks. Meanwhile, large-scale Viking raids continued. During 880 and 881, the Viking warriors suffered minor setbacks at the Battle of Thimeon (north of the Sambre River) and the Battle of Saucourt-en-Vimeu (near Abbeville). However, these did not change the general situation in favour of the Franks, who were still in the process of reorganizing their forces. During 879, a large Viking force, commanded by the Danish leader Godfrid, established a base at Ghent and rapidly assumed control over the whole of Frisia. In 884, at the Battle of Norditi, the Frisians decisively defeated the Scandinavian invaders, who were surprised by the incoming tide during the retreat that followed the clash and consequently suffered heavy losses. Following these events, an extensive system of dikes and seawalls was built in Frisia in order to protect the coastline from landings by Viking raiders.

In 885, the Vikings launched their largest attack against France, which resulted in the Siege of Paris. This time, some 300 warships with 12,000 warriors entered the mouth of the Seine, with the objective of creating a permanent settlement in northern France. Odo, Count of Paris, was well prepared to receive the invaders, confident that the two new low-lying foot bridges of his city (one made of wood and the other made of stone) blocked the passage of the Scandinavian ships. Before the arrival of the Vikings, he built a tower at the head of each bridge to improve the French defences against attacks coming from the banks of the Seine. After reaching Paris, the Vikings demanded the payment of a large sum of money, and when Odo refused to come to terms the siege operations began. The Vikings initially attacked the north-eastern tower, which protected the bridge made of wood. They were repulsed with heavy losses by the defenders, who employed a deadly mixture of hot wax and pitch to stop them. During the following days, the Vikings bombarded the city from siege engines and tried to destroy the bridge with fire, but all their attempts failed due to the sturdy resistance of the defenders. The Vikings maintained the siege for two months, building trenches and raiding the nearby countryside in search of supplies. In January 886, they tried to fill the river shallows with debris and plant matter in order to get around the besieged tower, but in the end they decided to change strategy and sent three burning warships against the wooden bridge in a bid to destroy it. The impact of the burning warships caused serious damage to the bridge, and a few days later, when heavy rains caused an overflow of the debris-filled river, the bridge collapsed. The north-eastern tower was now completely isolated, and although its remaining twelve defenders refused to surrender, they were all killed by the Scandinavians. After this success, the Vikings divided their forces into two parts: one remained on the eastern bank of the Seine in front of Paris, while the other sailed up-river to pillage as widely as possible. Le Mans, Chartres and Évreux were all attacked by the raiders, who also entered the course of the Loire River in order to sack more urban centres. In May 886, disease began to spread among the ranks of the defenders of Paris. The situation was desperate for the Franks, leaving Odo with no choice but to abandon the city in search of reinforcements. Having done so, he was later able to return to Paris at the head of a royal army and to enter the city over the stone-made bridge. By that time, a large number of the besiegers had already decided to return home, and the leadership of the Vikings who had remained around Paris was in the hands of a warlord named Rollo. Following another failed attack against the Ile de la Cité and after the arrival

Carolingian slinger. (*Photo and copyright by Novum Milites Francorum*)

Carolingian warlord wearing his civilian clothes. (*Photo and copyright by Novum Milites Francorum*)

Carolingian warlord displaying his sword with scabbard made of white leather.
(*Photo by Julien Souris, copyright by Gisna Missi Dominici*)

of the substantial Frankish reinforcements, Rollo finally accepted the payment of 700 pounds of silver in exchange for leaving Paris. Odo, who had been able to save the city thanks to his efforts, became King of France in 888. Although Paris was now safe, the Viking raids in France continued during the following decades. They were mostly directed against Normandy, where the Scandinavians were finally able to create some permanent settlements around their naval bases.

In 911, the King of France, Charles the Simple, decided to sign a treaty with the Viking raiders who had settled within the borders of his realm. The Treaty of Saint-Clair-sur-Epte established the new Duchy of Normandy under the guidance of the Viking leader Rollo. According to its terms, the Vikings who were already settled in Normandy became vassals of the French monarch in exchange for being permitted to create their own semi-autonomous country in northern France. The Vikings were given all the Norman lands located between the Epte River and the sea, along with Brittany, which, as we have seen, had never been under the firm control of the French monarchy; thus – at least temporarily – the rulers of France decided to not exert their authority over the region. In exchange for receiving a new homeland for his followers, Rollo guaranteed his loyalty to Charles the Simple and promised that his warriors would protect French territory from the incursions of any other Scandinavian raiders. The Treaty of Saint-Clair-sur-Epte contained various other conditions that the Vikings had to respect: first of all, they were to adopt the Christian faith as their new religion; in addition, they were to respect the central authority of the French monarchs in certain specific administrative fields. Considering that feudalism was developing in France during these years, it could be said that the compromise worked out between Rollo and Charles the Simple was nothing other than the stipulation of a feudal contract between two parties that had very little respect for each other. To seal the treaty, Rollo agreed to be baptized and to marry Gisela, a legitimate daughter of Charles the Simple. Over time, an increasing number of Scandinavians started to settle in the Duchy of Normandy. These, initially called Northmen by the French, soon started to be known as Normans.

The early years of the Viking presence in Normandy were not easy, the Normans having to abandon paganism and learn how to speak French. The fusion between their culture and the local one, however, soon started to have positive results. Many Scandinavian warriors, for example, married French women, and thus new Norman families were created. The former Vikings generally had positive relations with the French living inside and outside the borders of their territories. Nevertheless, they did fight on several occasions against the Bretons, who did not accept that their country had been assigned to their former allies. Being the most warlike vassals of the French monarchy, Rollo and his warlords soon started to expand their territorial possessions by moving westward. In 927, the Viking leader, who was later considered to be the first Duke of Normandy, was succeeded by his son, William Longsword. William was quite favourable to the Gallicization of his followers and had a great opinion of the contemporary French institutions. For these reasons, soon after assuming power, William had to face a rebellion mounted by some of his warlords who wanted to preserve the Viking identity of their community. The son of Rollo, however, crushed the revolt and later demonstrated himself to be a quite capable ruler. Taking advantage of the internal conflicts that continued to ravage the Kingdom of France, he convinced the central government to assign him some other lands that became part of the Duchy of Normandy: the areas of Avranches and the Cotentin Peninsula (which had previously been part of Brittany), as well as the Channel Islands. The Bretons, however, continued to fight to preserve their independence and mounted a strong resistance. William and his Normans, thanks to their military superiority, won a series of clashes against the Bretons and razed to the ground most of the enemy fortifications. During the last years of William's rule, the Normans were heavily involved in the civil wars fought in France between the various feudal lords, which usually determined the ascendancy of new monarchs. William's most fierce enemy was Arnulf of Flanders, who attacked the Duchy of Normandy and formed an alliance with the Bretons. They were thus able to reconquer – at least temporarily – several of their territories that had been conquered by the Normans. William Longsword was killed in an ambush – probably organized by Arnulf – in 942. He was succeeded by his son, Richard, who later became known as Richard I. The new Norman ruler was just a boy and he soon came under the control of his father's enemies, Louis IV of France and Arnulf of Flanders, who wanted to eradicate the Norman presence in northern France because they considered it as extremely dangerous for the political stability of the country. The young Richard was taken away from Normandy and placed in the custody of the Count of Ponthieu. Meanwhile, Louis IV tried to divide the Duchy of Normandy in two and to assign these to some of his most trusted allies. The French monarch, however, was too weak from a military point of view to reach his ambitious objective of retaking Normandy. Indeed, the Normans rebelled against him and obtained the release of their young but legitimate ruler. In 946, Richard formed an alliance with the Vikings who were active in other areas of France and went to war against Louis IV. The king was defeated and captured by the Normans, but was released after having formally recognized Richard as the legitimate Duke of Normandy. Soon after these events, Richard I formed an alliance with the main enemy of Louis IV, Hugh, the Count of Paris. Hugh had ambitions to become the new King of France, for which he needed the support of the Normans. In 947, Richard of Normandy and Hugh of Paris were attacked by Louis of France and

Carolingian warlord wearing his civilian clothes.
(*Photo by Julien Souris, copyright by Gisna Missi Dominici*)

Lombard heavy cavalryman equipped with a full set of lamellar armour, in perfect nomadic style. (*Photo by Sebastian Wesche-Bachmann, copyright by Stephan Becker*)

Arnulf of Flanders. Against all odds, Richard and Hugh prevailed. Their victory led to a long period of peace and stability for the Duchy of Normandy, during which Richard I transformed his domain into the most cohesive and powerful of France's feudal principalities. In 987, the son of Hugh of Paris, Hugh Capet, became the new monarch of France, initiating the new Capetian dynasty.

Chapter 8

Weapons and Tactics

During the third century AD, the traditional military equipment of the Germanic warriors started to change in a significant way. The nobles, for example, began equipping themselves with helmets and simple cuirasses made of chainmail. At the same time, new types of offensive weapons were also introduced. Germanic helmets were of a model technically known as spangenhelm: the term is clearly of Germanic origins, since '*spangen*' refers to the metal strips that formed the framework of this kind of helmet, while '*helm*' simply means 'helmet'. The characteristic metal strips of a spangenhelm connected between three and six steel or bronze plates. These made up a framework that had a conical design, which curved with the shape of the head and culminated in a point. The front of the helmet generally included a nasal, but spangenhelms could also incorporate a piece of chainmail for protection of the neck (which formed a sort of aventail). Some surviving examples of this kind of helmet also include a form of eye-protection, with a shape that resembles modern eyeglass frames; a few examples even include a full facial mask. Older spangenhelms often had cheek-flaps made of metal or leather. The spangenhelm offered effective protection for the head and was relatively easy to produce. It could feature heavy decorations, especially if the helmet belonged to a rich warrior. Many surviving examples have evidence of decorative silvering or are covered by costly silver-gilt sheathing. Helmets of senior warlords could be decorated with several glass gems that were located on the bowl and on the cheekpieces. Cuirasses could be of the *lorica hamata* or *lorica squamata* type, the former being more common to find among the western Germani and the latter being popular among the eastern Germani. The *lorica hamata*, or chainmail, comprised alternating rows of closed washer-like rings punched from iron sheets and rows of riveted rings made from drawn wire that ran horizontally, which produced very flexible, reliable and strong armour. Each ring had an inner diameter of about 5mm and an outer diameter of about 7mm. Up to 30,000 rings went into the manufacture of one *lorica hamata*, and the estimated production time for this type of cuirass was two months. Although labour-intensive to manufacture, this kind of armour, with good maintenance, could be used by a warrior for several decades. It was common for the *lorica hamata* to cover as far as the thighs or the knees, and its sleeves could be either long or short. The *lorica squamata*, or scale armour, was made up of small metal scales sewn to a fabric backing. The individual scales (*squamae*) could be of iron or bronze. The metal was generally not very thick, a common range being between 0.5mm and 0.8mm. Since the scales overlapped in every direction, however, the multiple layers gave good protection. Scales could have rounded, pointed or flat bottoms with the corners clipped off at an angle. They could be flat, slightly domed or have a raised midrib/edge. The scales were wired or laced together in horizontal rows that were then laced or sewn to the backing. Therefore, each scale had between four and twelve holes: two or more at each side for wiring to the next scale in the row, one or two at the top for fastening to the backing and sometimes one or two at the bottom to secure the scales to the backing or to each other. Occasionally, the *squamae* could be tinned (covered with a thin layer of tin). Before AD 200, both the helmets and the cuirasses described above were used only by the richest warriors, but as time progressed the great majority of Germanic warriors started to be equipped with these defensive elements.

The eastern Germani, in particular, were heavily influenced by the steppe peoples living on their borders, and as a consequence they developed bodies of heavy cavalry within their military forces. These were made up of cataphracts, who wore full armour and were armed with a specific model of cavalry lance known as the contus. This lance was about 4 metres long and had to be wielded with two hands, while the cavalryman directed the horse using his knees, which made it a specialist weapon that required a great deal of training and good horsemanship to wield effectively. Initially, only highly trained cavalry, such as those fielded by the steppe peoples, could use this lance in an effective manner. The contus was reputedly a weapon of great power, especially if compared to other cavalry spears of the time. The great length of the lance was probably the origin of its name, since the Greek word '*kontus*' meant 'oar' or 'barge-pole'. The Roman cavalry adopted the contus on a massive scale, like the Germani, after facing the Sarmatian heavy cavalry in battle. Apparently, the eastern Germani also adopted the composite bow of the steppe peoples' light cavalry, albeit on a small scale. This was made from horn, wood and sinew, which were laminated together. The horn was on the belly of the bow, facing the archer, while the sinew was on the outer side of the wooden core. This gave the bow its shape and dimensional stability. When the bow was drawn, the sinew (stretched on the outside) and horn (compressed on the inside) stored more energy than the wood for the same length of bow. The construction of a composite bow was a very complex process: it required more varieties of material than a simple wooden bow and much more time. Such weapons were often made from multiple pieces joined together with animal glue in V-shaped splices. Pieced construction allowed the use of woods with different mechanical properties for the bending and non-bending sections of the bow: the

Lombard lamellar helmet of the Niederstotzingen type.
(*Photo and copyright by Sebastian Wesche-Bachmann*)

Nice example of a Carolingian nasal helmet. (*Photo and copyright by Novum Milites Francorum*)

Display of Carolingian helmets; all are characterized by segmented construction and have an aventail of chainmail on the back. (*Photo and copyright by Hiwisca – Eine Familia in der Karolingerzeit*)

wood of the bending part of the limb had to endure intense shearing stress. A thin layer of horn was glued onto what would be the belly of the bow, which could store more energy than wood in compression. Goat and sheep horn were commonly used for this purpose. The sinew, soaked in animal glue, was then laid in layers on the back of the bow, and the strands of sinew were oriented along the length of the bow. The sinew was normally obtained from the lower legs and back of wild deer or domestic ungulates. Sinew would extend farther than wood, again allowing more energy storage. Hide glue was used to attach layers of sinew to the back of the bow and to attach the horn belly to the wooden core. Almost all composite bows were recurve ones, as this design gave higher draw-weight in the early stages of the archer's draw.

During the period of the Great Migrations that ultimately caused the fall of the Western Roman Empire, three new offensive weapons were added to the traditional panoply of the Germanic warriors: the *angon*, the *seax* and the *francisca*. The *angon* was a heavy javelin with a barbed head and a long narrow socket or shank, which was made of iron and was mounted on a wooden haft. The barbs of the head were designed to lodge in the enemy shields so that it could not be removed. The long iron shank prevented the head from being cut from the shaft. The *angon* was likely designed, similarly to the Roman *pilum* javelin, for the purpose of disabling enemy shields

Carolingian infantryman wearing a very simple form of segmented helmet.
(*Photo by Julien Souris, copyright by Floriferum Bucler*)

Carolingian infantryman wearing a helmet and scale armour protecting the upper legs. (*Photo and copyright by Jurgen Ritter*)

and thus of leaving enemy combatants vulnerable. The shaft could be decorated, and sometimes iron or bronze rings were fitted onto it to mark the centre of balance and thus the best place to hold the weapon. The *seax* (also known as a *scramasax*) was a short sword, mostly – but not only – used by the cavalry, that came into use

Carolingian infantryman carrying his massive round shield on his back, in order to have some additional protection. (*Photo and copyright by Jurgen Ritter*)

among the eastern Germani and was later adopted by a great number of Germanic warriors. Its name meant 'knife' in the Germanic language, and apparently the term 'Saxon' derived from it. This short sword had a large and single-edged blade, which had a tang in the centreline, that was inserted into an organic hilt made of wood or horn. The *seax* was worn horizontally inside a scabbard made of leather, which was attached to the waist belt of each warrior (inside the scabbard, the edge of the blade was pointing upwards). Sometimes, a small side-knife, with its own leather scabbard, was attached on the front of the short sword's scabbard. The *francisca*, like the *seax*, first came into use among the eastern Germani but later became the national weapon of the Franks, whose name apparently gave birth to the term '*francisca*'. This weapon was a light axe, mostly designed to be thrown from a distance. It had an arch-shaped head, which widened towards the cutting edge and terminated in a prominent point at both the upper and lower corners. The top of the head was S-shaped or convex, with the lower portion curving inward and forming an elbow with the short wooden haft. According to ancient sources, the Germani threw their light axes with incredible accuracy, meaning the *francisca* was particularly feared by their opponents. During the period of the Great Migrations, the shields and swords of the Germanic warriors changed considerably. A new model of oval or round shield came into use, which was either dished (bowl-shaped) or flat. The oval/round shield was much larger than the models used previously and was constructed in a different way: it was made of solid planks instead of plywood and was supported by a double grip (at the elbow and the hand). The new shield was about 110cm high and 90cm wide, being constructed with 1cm-thick wood planks, and was covered and bound with leather. In addition, differently from the previous models, it had a reinforcement made of metal on the external edge and could be decorated with many bronze or iron fittings on the external surface. A hollow iron or bronze boss covered the central hand grip.

The Germanic peoples were famous for the high quality of their offensive weapons, which had a specific social function in Europe during the Early Middle Ages, as bearing arms was both a right and a duty of the free men and distinguished them from the slaves. As a result, weapons were seen as status symbols, and their quality and ornamentation reflected the economic capabilities of their owner. Swords, in the Germanic world, had a great symbolic value because producing them was extremely difficult and costly. Only the most prominent warlords could have a sword of high quality, meaning that such weapons were usually handed down from generation to generation. Most of the Germanic warriors gave a name to their swords and had a special relationship with them, since they also acted like amulets and their symbolism was strongly linked to the very soul of their owner. Elegant shapes and rich ornamentations were typical of the aristocrats' weaponry, but most of the middle-class warriors also had no hesitation in spending large sums of money in order to have the best arms. In Germanic Europe, the processes of forging and tempering were performed by specialized craftsmen and were surrounded by a web of myth. The use of the best materials and control of the temperature during the various productive phases were key factors behind the creation of an effective weapon. Germanic swords were often decorated with symbols that had a religious or cultural meaning, which were reproduced as patterns that were laid into the iron during forging and became visible when the external surface of the weapon was polished and etched. A good sword blade had to be flexible but should not be easily broken. In addition, a sword's edge had to keep its sharpness for as long as possible. These main characteristics were obtained by placing hard steel on the sword's edge and soft iron along the middle of the blade. Producing a sword of good quality was an extremely long process, which had many phases: forging, folding, hammering and forging again. Reworking steel and iron at high temperatures rendered them homogenous and thus reduced the risk of the weapon shattering under the strain of use.

The standard Germanic sword was a single-handed weapon that was designed to leave one of the warrior's hands free in order to hold his shield. Its hilt consisted of three parts: back-hilt, grip and fore-hilt. Sometimes, the latter was made up of two parts, the hindmost one of which was commonly known as the pommel. Most of the hilts were made of iron, but sometimes they could be manufactured from bronze. The total length of a Germanic sword was some 80–85cm, while the average length of the blade was 65–70cm. Blades were about 4–5cm wide and their weight was restricted towards the point, which was obtained by tapering the blades both in breadth and in thickness towards the point. As a result of this manufacturing process, the blade's thickness was 6mm near the hilt and 2mm at the point of the sword. To reduce the weight further and increase flexibility, a groove was forged and ground out along the middle of the blade. The centre of gravity of the weapon was near the hilt, which made it quite easy to handle. Several swords, especially those belonging to the richest individuals, had decorative inscriptions on the blade and decorated hilts. All swords were carried in leather-bound wooden scabbards that were suspended from a strap across the right shoulder. Like the scabbard, the hilt was also made of an organic material, such as horn or antler.

Most of the common Germanic warriors did not have a sword, instead being equipped quite simply with just a spear and a shield. Germanic spears were produced in two main versions: throwing spears and thrusting spears. The heads of the throwing spears had an average length of 20cm, while those of the thrusting spears had a standard length of 70cm. Spear heads consisted of two parts: the blade and the socket. The wooden shaft was fixed into the socket with one or two nails.

Front view of a Carolingian round shield.
(*Photo and copyright by Hiwisca – Eine Familia in der Karolingerzeit*)

Occasionally, spears could also have two projections on the side of the socket that were known as wings and were used to remove the spear more easily from enemy shields. The back end of the shaft could sometimes be capped with a metal ferrule. Spear blades could be of two different kinds. The first, and older, model of blade was forged with a herringbone pattern along the middle and had curved edges, and blended inconspicuously into the socket. The socket tended towards a square internal cross-section and was decorated with longitudinal grooves. The second, newer model of blade had nearly straight edges (which ended in an angle at the base) and a marked narrowing as it merged into the socket. Its socket was round in cross-section and

Back view of a Carolingian round shield.
(*Photo and copyright by Hiwisca – Eine Familia in der Karolingerzeit*)

could be decorated with inlaid precious metal. Wings were very common on the first model but quite rare on the second. The wings had another important practical function in addition to easing the extraction of the spear from enemy shields: they could be used for hooking onto the edge of an enemy shield and thus for opening the way for a strike at an enemy warrior. The wooden shaft of the thrusting spear was longer than that of the throwing spear; the former was 2.5–3 metres long, while the latter was about 1.5 metres long. The diameter of all shafts was about 2.5cm and

Display of Carolingian swords. (*Photo and copyright by Hiwisca – Eine Familia in der Karolingerzeit*)

sometimes narrowed towards the back end. In general, throwing spears were less popular than thrusting ones.

With the beginning of the Viking incursions in Western Europe, axes started to become much more popular. They could belong to two different categories: broad-bladed axes and bearded axes. Broad-bladed axes had a blade length of 20–30cm and were specifically designed for combat use. Their head could be either L-shaped or M-shaped. The blade was thin but wide and had pronounced horns at both the toe and the heel of the bit. L-shaped axes tended to be smaller and had the toe of the bit swept forward for superior shearing capability. M-shaped axes were bigger and had a more symmetrical toe and heel. Most of the battle axes were made from wrought iron but had a reinforced bit made of carbon steel that was placed near the edge in order to provide the weapon with a devastating cutting capability. The average weight of a battle axe was 1.5kg. The wooden haft had a standard length of 1–1.5 metres and was linked to the head with a cap that protected its end from the rigours of combat. On most occasions, the haft was made from ash or oak. The bearded axe was single-handed and was mostly employed as a throwing weapon. Its name derived from the hook or beard, the lower portion of the head's bit that extended the cutting edge below the width of the butt (providing a wide cutting surface while keeping the overall weight of the weapon low). The peculiar design of the bearded axe allowed its user to grip the haft directly behind the head, which was of great use when throwing the weapon. Bows were not very popular among Germanic warriors, especially in Western Europe, being employed for hunting but only rarely seen on battlefields. Germanic bows were made from yew, ash or elm; they had a draw force of 100 pounds and an effective range of 200 metres. From a technical point of view, they were longbows since they were made from a single piece of wood. This was either cut from the centre of a tree trunk or worked from a branch of suitable shape and size. The overall height of a Germanic bow generally corresponded to that of its user. When not in use, a bow was almost straight, but when strung, it was nearly D-shaped in cross-section. Arrow shafts were cut from thin shoots created by coppicing the appropriate trees, while bowstrings were made of linen thread looped and bound into a cord. Arrowheads could be of three different kinds: blade-shaped, spike-shaped and chisel-shaped. Spike-shaped arrowheads were specifically designed for combat use, with the other two types also used for hunting. Each arrowhead was fixed with a tang to its shaft, which had feathers applied at the nock end away from the head and was some 65–75cm long.

Until the end of the Carolingian period, the most important component of a Germanic warrior's defensive panoply was his shield, which had a distinctive round shape and was quite flat, having a hole in the middle where a wooden carrying handle was mounted crossways on the inside. A dome of plate iron, the boss, was nailed over the hole on the outside in order to protect the hand. This had the shape of a straight-sided cone with a flanged base. Four holes in the flange allowed the boss to be riveted to the shield's face. Sometimes, decorative fittings made of copper alloy or gold could be applied on the external surface of the bosses. Carolingian-era shields had a diameter of 80–95cm and were made up of seven or eight planks glued together edge to edge in order to form a single plate. The thickness of the planks was 7–8mm near the middle of the shield and 5–6mm near the edge. A layer of rawhide (usually cow-hide) was glued onto the whole of the shield's front and back, and was held in position by stitch holes that were placed round the edge where a band of rawhide was folded round and sewn for reinforcement. The presence of the rawhide reduced the risk of the wood splitting and helped in stopping enemy arrows. Linden softwood was usually chosen to build shields, which had an average weight of 7kg. When not in combat, Germanic warriors carried their shields on their back, thanks to a leather belt that was attached to the wooden handle. Shields were frequently reinforced with an iron strip around the rim, which was particularly useful during hand-to-hand

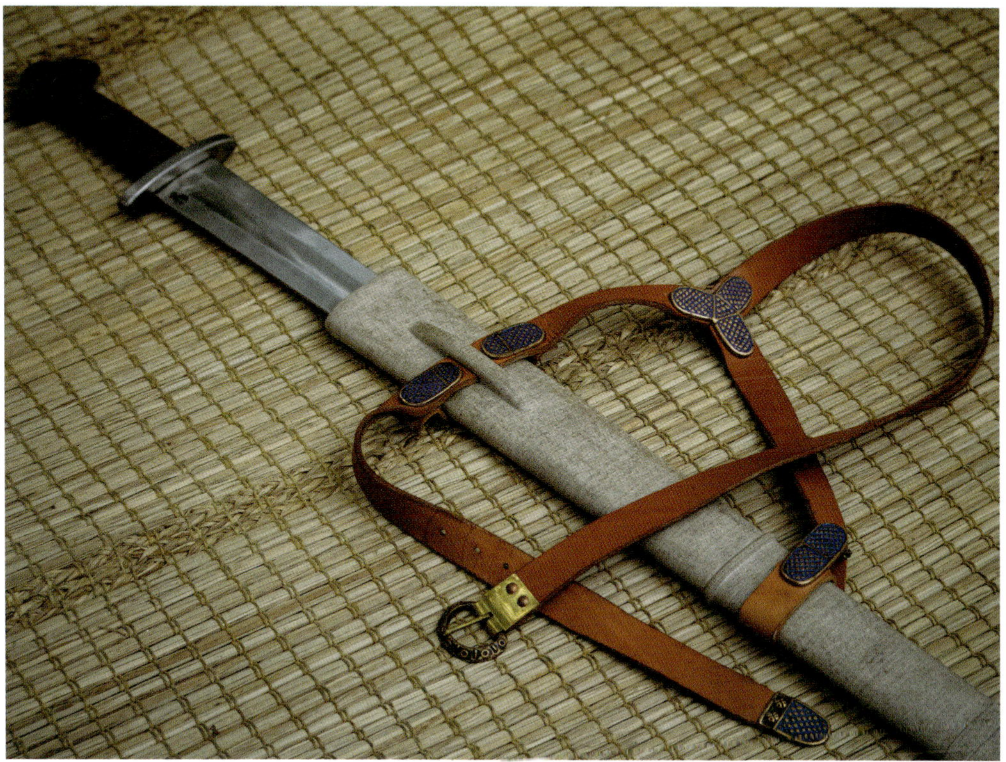

Nice example of a Carolingian sword. (*Photo and copyright by Novum Milites Francorum*)

fighting. Most of the round shields were painted in a single colour, but several were decorated with specific designs. Simple crosses and sacred animals and creatures (such as crows or dragons) were the most common designs. Quite frequently, rich warlords could ornate the external surface of their shields with decorative fittings made of copper alloy or gold.

The everyday dress of a Germanic warrior consisted of two main elements: the cloak and the tunic. The cloak was rectangular in shape, being about 2.5 metres long and 1.5 metres wide. Made of woollen yarn, it was usually pinned at the right shoulder and hung to about knee-length. The cloak was kept in position thanks to a metal brooch known as a fibula, which could be produced in many different patterns. Initially, most of the brooches were cruciform and had a bowed section in order to allow material to be pulled through between the body of the wearer and the back-mounted pin. Over time, however, new and smaller brooches with a simpler circular shape became increasingly popular. The tunic, like the cloak, was made of woollen yarn. It was usually worn belted at the waist in such a way as to raise the hem to the knees. Sometimes, however, tunics could be worn without a belt, in which case their hems would hang to the calves. Most Germanic tunics were long-sleeved, reaching

Detail of the handle of a Carolingian sword. (*Photo and copyright by De vita aetate carolingorum*)

well down over the fingers, but they were usually worn pulled or folded back to the wrist during the warmer months. The neck of each tunic had either a square or circular opening for the head, which was generally reinforced with a coloured placket. This opening could be closed either by a drawstring or by a brooch/bead. Both the

Different versions of Carolingian *seax* short sword.
(*Photo and copyright by Hiwisca – Eine Familia in der Karolingerzeit*)

cloaks and the tunics could be produced in a variety of bright colours, although plain hues were extremely popular among the common warriors. Aristocratic warlords wore garments heavily ornamented with coloured plackets and/or decorative embroidering on the edges. Leggings were quite common for warriors during the early years of the Germanic presence in Western Europe, usually taking the form of trousers with the feet sewn into them and slits at the ankles that allowed them to be put on more easily. Over time, separate leggings and hose became increasingly popular. Leggings had the form of trousers that were sometimes allowed to hang loose around the ankles. Quite frequently, long fabric strips could be wound closely to the calf, in order to act as puttees; these were popular for campaign use, but could also be worn during everyday life. The leg bindings were known as '*winniga*' and usually covered most of the leg, protecting both the leg and the trousers from cold and dirt. The footwear of the Germanic warriors was very simple, consisting of shoes made of cow hide. All the belts worn by the Germanic warriors were made of leather and were usually about 2.5cm wide. The buckles and the strap-ends of the belts were made of copper alloy and could be heavily decorated if worn by aristocratic warlords. The standard headgear of the Germanic warriors when not in combat was the Phrygian cap, which was made of wool or felt. This had a characteristic forward-drooping peak and had been a symbol of a man's free status since the days of the Roman Empire. The Phrygian cap was used as a type of fatigue headgear by commoners, but it was popular too among the nobles, who wore decorated versions of it.

Carolingian *francisca* axe and *seax* short swords. (*Photo and copyright by Novum Milites Francorum*)

Points of Carolingian spears and javelins.
(*Photo and copyright by Hiwisca – Eine Familia in der Karolingerzeit*)

Carolingian bow and quiver. (*Photo and copyright by Hiwisca – Eine Familia in der Karolingerzeit*)

The military tactics of the Germani changed alongside the equipment that they used in battle. At the beginning of the period taken into account in this book, the Germanic warriors preferred fighting in tight formations stretched out in lines in order to overlap their shields and thus form a defensive wall in case of enemy attack. A line could be densely packed or sparse, with gaps between the fighters, depending on how long it had to be and on how many warriors were available. The depth of a defensive formation was usually between five and eight lines. The most experienced and better equipped warriors were deployed in the front line, the main task of those in the back lines being simply to plug gaps in the front line. Shoulder-to-shoulder shield walls of spear-carrying warriors were an effective defensive formation, especially when supported by a number of archers who could fire their arrows from behind the main battle line. All the Germanic peoples defended in line and attacked in column on the battlefield. A standard battle fought in Germanic Europe began with the drawing up of the lines and the inspirational speeches of the most prominent warlords. Once these had been completed, a battle cry was raised and one or both shield walls advanced. Before the formation of the attacking columns, the two confronting sides fired arrows and threw javelins at each other, while slingers could also occasionally participate in this phase of the clash by throwing their stones from long distance. At this point of the battle, champions fighters could come out from the ranks of their army to challenge the enemy warriors. As a result, before the main clash could start, duels between elite warriors usually took place in the strip of land between the opposing armies. After the end of the duels, one of the two sides charged in column formation, while the other formed a horizontal shield wall. The ensuing hand-to-hand melee fighting was extremely violent but often lasted for just a few minutes, both sides striving to open a gap in the formation of the enemy by pushing with their shields. A gap might be opened quite easily, but sometimes the

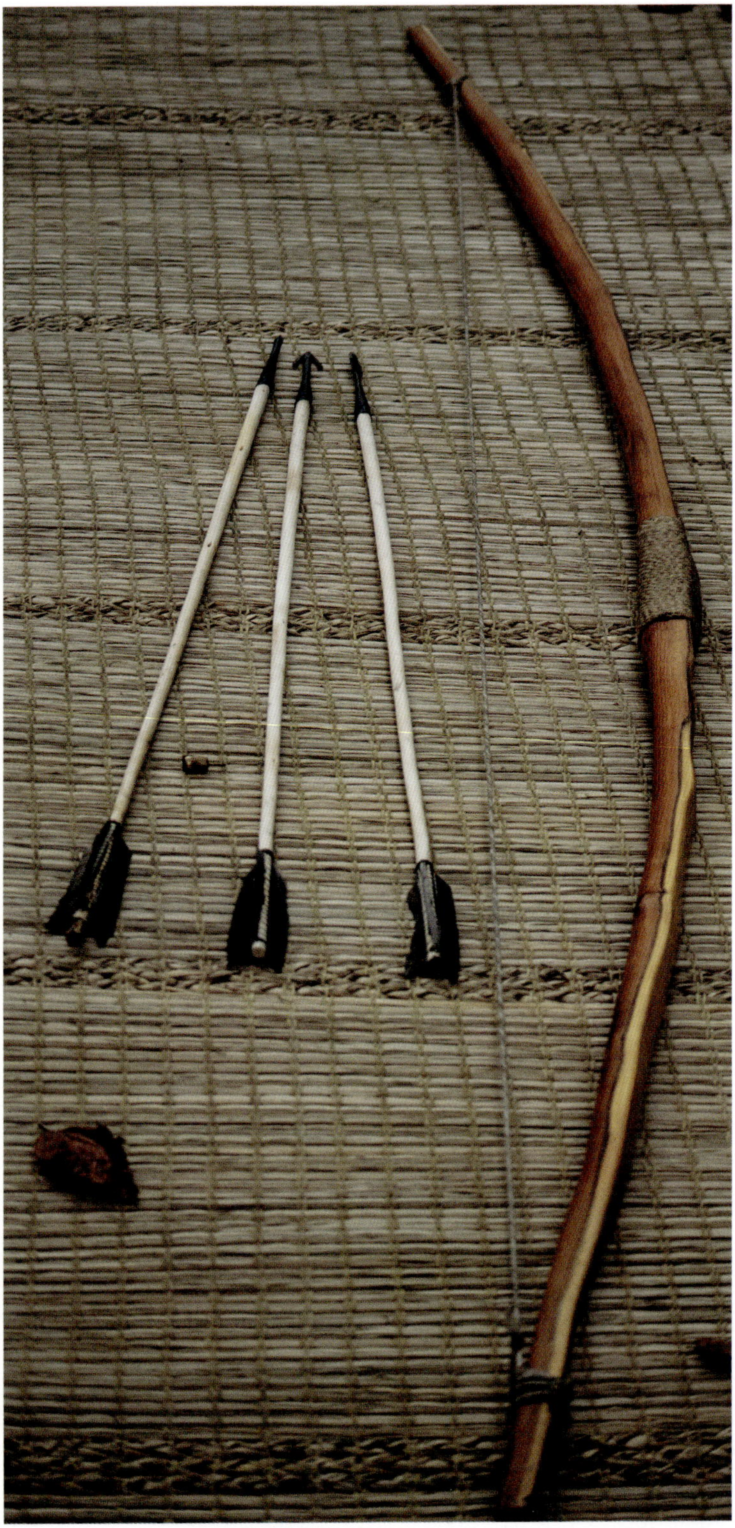

Carolingian bow and arrows. (*Photo and copyright by Novum Milites Francorum*)

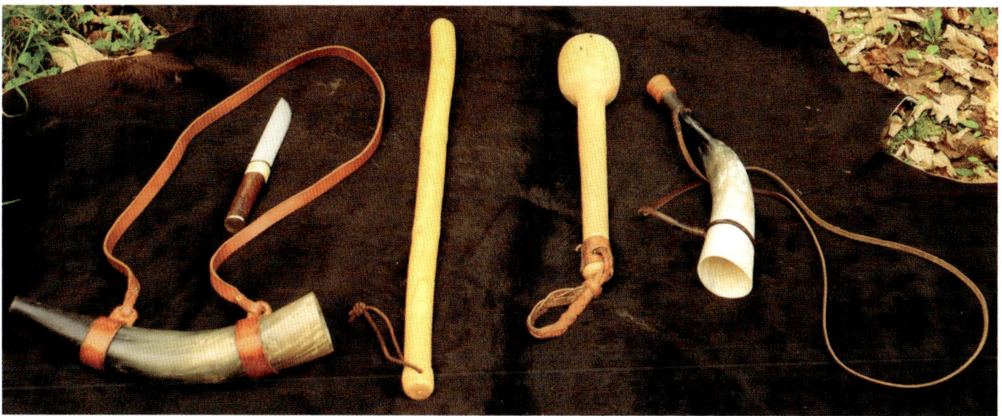

Carolingian horns and maces. (*Photo and copyright by Hiwisca – Eine Familia in der Karolingerzeit*)

Carolingian spurs. (*Photo and copyright by Novum Milites Francorum*)

close combat could last for hours. If neither line broke formation and fled, both sides would draw back to rest and more missiles would be exchanged before resuming hand-to-hand fighting. This would continue until one line broke through the other, maybe following the death of an important leader or the capture of a banner. The victors usually followed their routed enemies from the battlefield in close pursuit and killed as many opponents as possible. Generally speaking, Germanic military confrontations were extremely violent and caused severe losses to the armies involved in them. On several occasions, however, they were not decisive in determining the outcome of a conflict.

When attacking, a column was deployed in a very aggressive tactical formation known as a boar's snout. This was a wedge formation, which worked in a very simple but effective way. It had the shape of an equilateral triangle, with the commander being the apex. The best warriors were deployed near the apex, while those with little combat experience were placed at the back of the formation. The chosen warriors of the first ranks followed the movements of their commander very closely and were in turn followed by the warriors of the other ranks, as a result of which the formation could move very rapidly and was extremely flexible. If stopped by the resistance of the enemy, the attacking wedge rapidly turned into a more solid rectangle, with the warriors of the rear ranks advancing to support those who were near the vertex. The boar's snout was the perfect formation to attack an enemy wall of shields at a particular point, but was exposed to counter-attacks on its flanks. After breaking through the enemy line, the warriors of the wedge formation attacked their enemies on both the right and the left from the rear. All the tactical movements of the Germanic armies were coordinated through the presence of horn blowers and standard-bearers on the battlefield. Long horns were blown to transmit orders, while the standard-bearers indicated the position of a formation's leader with their banners. Germanic military forces carried small triangular banners as well as impressive standards of the *draco* 'windsock' type. The *draco* had the form of a dragon, with open wolf-like jaws containing several metal tongues. The hollow head of the dragon was made of metal and was mounted on a pole, with a long fabric tube fixed to the rear. When used in battle, the *draco* was held up aloft, where it filled with air and made a shrill sound as the wind passed through its metal tongues. It was a perfect example of psychological warfare, filling opponents with fear, especially during the early phases of a pitched battle.

Bibliography

Anderson, E.B., *Cataphracts: Knights of the Ancient Eastern Empires* (Pen & Sword, 2016).

Bachrach, B.S., *Merovingian Military Organization 481–751* (University of Minnesota Press, 1972).

Baldi, M., *L'Esercito Longobardo 568–774* (Editrice Militare Italiana, 1991).

Barker, P. and Heath, I., *The Armies and Enemies of Imperial Rome* (Wargames Research Group, 1981).

Blair, J., *Building Anglo-Saxon England* (Princeton University Press, 2018).

Breay, C. and Story, J., *Anglo-Saxon Kingdoms: Art, Word, War* (British Library Publishing, 2018).

Cassard, J.C., *Le Siècle Des Vikings En Bretagne* (Editions Jean-Paul Gisserot, 1996).

Fleming, R., *Britain after Rome: the Fall and Rise, 400 to 1070* (Penguin, 2011).

Goldsworthy, A., *The Fall of the West: The Slow Death of the Roman Superpower* (Weidenfeld & Nicolson, 2009).

Gorelik, K., *Warriors of Eurasia* (Montvert Publishing, 1995).

Gravett, C., *Norman Knight 950–1204* (Osprey Publishing, 1994).

Harrison, M., *Viking Hersir 793–1066* (Osprey Publishing, 1993).

Heath, I., *Armies of Feudal Europe 1066–1300* (Wargames Research Group, 1989).

Heath, I., *Armies of the Dark Ages 600–1066* (Wargames Research Group, 1980).

Heath, I., *The Vikings* (Osprey Publishing, 1985).

Hjardar, K. and Vegard, V., *Vikings at War* (Casemate, 2019).

Hooper, N. and Bennett, M., *Warfare in the Middle Ages 768–1487* (Cambridge University Press, 1996).

Macdowall, S. and McBride, A., *Germanic Warrior AD 236–568* (Osprey Publishing, 1996).

Nicolle, D., *Carolingian Cavalryman 768–987* (Osprey Publishing, 2005).

Nicolle, D., *Romano-Byzantine Armies 4th–9th Centuries* (Osprey Publishing, 1992).

Nicolle, D., *The Age of Charlemagne* (Osprey Publishing, 1984).

Nicolle, D., *The Normans* (Osprey Publishing, 1987).

Wilcox, P. and Embleton, G., *Rome's Enemies 1: Germanics and Dacians* (Osprey Publishing, 1982).

Winroth, A., *The Age of the Vikings* (Princeton University Press, 2014).

Wise, T., *Saxon, Viking and Norman* (Osprey Publishing, 1979).

The Re-enactors who Contributed to this Book

De vita aetate carolingorum

'De vita aetate carolingorum' is part of the RCF (Re-enactment Combat Fighting) associations 'Equites Dragonis' and 'Familia Carolina' in the Lauresham Open Air Museum in Lorsch. The 'Familia Carolina' enlivens, among other things, the houses in the open-air laboratory. For visitors to the museum, they make a significant contribution to gaining authentic access to the clothing of the early Middle Ages and of the Carolingians, to individual textile techniques but also to a wide variety of crafts. Ultimately, alongside the research and educational work, we are one of Lauresham's quality features.

Contacts:
Facebook:https://www.facebook.com/people/De-vita-aetate-carolingorum/100063198971038/?locale=en_GB&paipv=0&eav=AfZz3ViAzU1TWWzSoH6S2TC8SxzXfI_mXslUG80QUad__dxS6uhHvtZF2K_kI9huyfA&_rdr
Email: feba@gmx.at

Hiwisca – Eine Familia in der Karolingerzeit

'Hiwisca', another word for the Latin 'familia', means a group of people with a common interest and relationship - not necessarily kinship. Our group recreates and enacts a traveling party of the Carolingian epoch around AD 800. Traveling at this time was a risky venture: while roads and paths were policed, wild animals like wolves or bears and especially bandits and marauders were a constant threat. The safety of numbers was usually a good reason to join a traveling party; these groups could comprise dozens of individuals of different social extractions and occupations, like nobles and their armed retainers, traders, clergy and journeying craftsmen. 'Hiwisca' makes an appearance several times a year at museum events with a Carolingian topic. We are always happy to inform interested visitors about our equipment like pottery, clothing or weapons as well as about history, politics, law and the social system at the time of Charlemagne.

Contacts:
Facebook: https://www.facebook.com/people/Hiwisca-Eine-Familia-in-der-Karolingerzeit/100063239828035/?locale=zh_TW&paipv=0&eav=AfZDyhqVqMaj4NoZ86q3z5mRSHKMM4UQndh7KjCjn0LSuI5Pl_oM28k8A0rkqwrkccE&_rdr
Email: info@ask-alamannen.de

Hunjos Arbi

'Hunjos Arbi' means something like 'The Heirs of the Huns', in Gothic language. This refers to those Germanic kingdoms that emerged stronger from the alliance with the Huns and continued and spread the cultural peculiarities of the Asian equestrian nomads in Eastern and Central Europe. We want to tell this story of the Goths, Thuringians, Herulians, Gepids and others in our re-enactment group and illustrate it to an audience. 'Hunjos Arbi' is an international group association that brings together various re-enactment groups dedicated to these cultures under one unifying name. The aim is to embody a culturally uniform image and to present connecting, specific archaeological and cultural features at re-enactment and museum events and in the media. Our association is made up of three main groups: 'Swarafulk' - Re-enactment of the Ostrogothic period from AD 450 to 550. They represent the Ostrogoths from the time of Hun rule, through the migrations in the Balkans, through the destruction of Odoacer, up to the establishment of the Ostrogoth Kingdom in Italy and its end. 'Harjaz Toringem' - Re-enactment of the Thuringian Kingdom from AD 450 to 531. Their representations focus mainly on reconstructions of the area of the Thuringian Kingdom from the end of the Attila period, through the establishment of an independent kingdom up to its destruction by the Franks in 531. They also deal with its lesser-known peripheral areas of the Warnen and Lombards. 'Heruli' - Re-enactment of the Heruli tribe from the time of Hun rule to the Kingdom of Rodulf in Moravia and Bohemia at the end of the fifth century. Their focus lies primarily in the Hun period, when the Herulians were part of the Huns' association of nations. Equestrian nomadic characteristics are the focus and shape the specific image of the Eastern peoples in Attila's time. 'Hunjos Arbi' as an association enables us to integrate other groups and individual performers who are dedicated to this topic and who are active in the period of migration and to expand our repertoire. We see it as our highest duty to carry out precise research into archaeological and historical sources in order to be able to present the most authentic picture possible. We produce the majority of our reconstructions by ourselves.

Contacts:
Facebook: https://www.facebook.com/p/Hunjos-Arbi-100063489643579/?paipv=0&eav=AfZHERsbcrmTI7LcRFV1IkIXd95mI9Q-KfAaAX2H1LzWjxRngv-9MxiWYU2JBELSAd4&_rdr
Email: info@swarafulk.de

Viatores

'Viatores' is a French living history group based in Toulouse, with branches in different parts of the country (Normandy, Brittany, Provence). It has been founded in 2021 by archeology-specialists Baptiste Legeron, Vincent Gonin and Antonin Chenel and by craftsman Jake Saunders, all four experienced living historians. Our main focus is on the mid-fifth century Visigoth dominions but we work on multiple periods. The common thread of all our projects is represented by the travellers of the past (nomads, pilgrims, mercenaries). 'Viatores' is now composed by a handful of enthusiasts working on different aspects of the ancient and medieval life (crafts of all sorts, war and combat, costume and calligraphy). We mostly work for museums and engage in private living history events too.

Contacts:
Facebook: https://www.facebook.com/viatores.lespetitspedestres/
Email: viatores.asso@gmail.com

Lupi Austrasiae

'Lupi Austrasiae' is a Belgian association that re-enacts the fifth century of the Merovingian age. We offer different mediation workshops (like weaving, forging, historical cooking, weapons and warfare) and we collaborate with some archaeological sites and events in Belgium and in the north of France in order to promote living history.

Contacts:
Facebook: https://www.facebook.com/LupiAustrasiae
Email: lupi.austrasiae@gmail.com

Toxandria Francorum

We are a rather small group, a family portraying sixth/seventh century life in the Low Countries, based in Flanders (Belgium); this region and its archaeological material has been our starting point. Our love and passion is to create old archaeological objects into replicas and bring them back to life, to see how they would have looked, how they would have felt and how they could have been used/worn and functioning during their lifetime approximately 1,400 years ago. Forging and leather work as well as sewing clothes are among our skills to bring these ancient objects and remnants back to life. We try to give a glimpse into life 1,400 years ago and keep the flame of 'living history' and this versatile period alive. A lot of research is involved, for example, in visualizing and interpreting the smallest leather fragments and thus making a reconstruction of a leather belt and this process applies to every single object to be reconstructed. Unfortunately, this historical period is not so well known to a larger public and yet it is an important period (back then and now archaeologically). Flanders is also covered with a multitude of Merovingian period finds and Merovingian period burial grounds, some better documented than others, with a number of discoveries having quite special backgrounds/origins. We identify under the name 'Toxandria Francorum' or 'Tehswandroz', a little background information about the choice of the name. To start, there is still some debate on what region specifically is meant by 'Toxandria' or even what this term means or indicates. Other known forms are Toxandrië, Texandrië, Taxandrië and Taxandria. Historically, the first century AD source of Pliny the Elder mentioned the Germanic people 'Texuandri', i.e. 'those who live south/on the right bank of the river Meuse or the river Rhine'. The Germanic words 'tehswa' and 'andra' would mean 'on the right bank' from a geographical point of view; this is likely in relation with the Batavians living further north. The Latin form Texuandri originates most likely from a Germanic (Batavian?) population or a combination of remnant groups whose living area was situated on the southern Dutch and neighbouring Northern Belgian sandy soils up to the Scheldt in the west. This area probably previously belonged to the territory of the Celtic Eburones.

Contacts:
Facebook: https://www.facebook.com/profile.php?id=100071801515778
Email: bert.tessens@gmail.com

Novum Milites Francorum

'Novum Milites Francorum' is a Dutch living history group that depicts life in the early ninth century in and around the modern Netherlands. We focus on portraying elite professional soldiers and their retinue in the Carolingian realm during the reign of Louis the Pious and try to show the public the full spectrum of soldierly life. Frequently, we can be seen guarding strategic points, marching through or honing and drilling our formations. Occasionally we veer from our martial course and explore different aspects of life such as pilgrimage, hunting and various crafts to enrich our understanding of life in the ninth century. Our depiction is based upon both archaeological and historical sources. Close examination of source material followed by discussion leads to an informed decision on specific pieces of our kit. Those who are familiar with this period recognize the problematic lack of evidence for a multitude of items. This scarce evidence often consists of some damaged finds or unclear drawings. However, we make choices based on the available sources and are always willing to change an item when new evidence presents itself. We can be found at events in archaeological open air museums and historical markets in and around the Netherlands. We try to give a narrative to the frequent fight-shows and enrich the experience of both participants and public with a bit of theatre. Connecting and sharing knowledge with fellow re-enactors and historical enthusiasts is one of our main goals. Secretly, we hope this book leads to more people discovering this fantastic period in history and want to become fellow Carolingians at the weekends.

Contacts:
Facebook: https://www.facebook.com/NovumMilitesFrancorum/
Email: hetbolwerklg@gmail.com

Index

Adelchis, 99
Alcuin of York, 133
Amalasuntha, 36
Ambrosius Aurelianus, 66, 70
Autari, 72

Bonifacius, 45

Caracalla, 1
Charles the Simple, 163
Childeric III, 90
Constantine III, 15

Desiderata, 78, 95, 99

Einhard, 133

Galla Placidia, 17, 19
Gelimer, 50, 52
Gratian, 59
Gudfred, 107, 109

Hilderic, 48, 50
Hugh Capet, 150, 166

Joannes, 17
Julian, 9

Magnentius, 59
Magnus Maximus, 59
Marcus, 59

Paul the Deacon, 133

Severus Alexander, 1
Syagrius, 79

Tassilo III, 105, 106
Totila, 40, 43, 44

Vitiges, 36, 38, 40
Vortigern, 61, 64

Zeno, 35